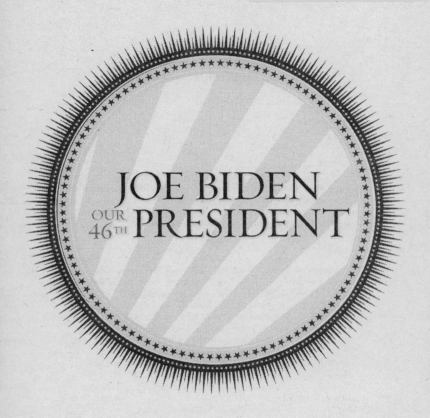

# JOE BIDEN
### OUR 46TH PRESIDENT

By Beatrice Gormley

ALADDIN
New York London Toronto Sydney New Delhi

*To my grandsons, Anthony and James*

ALADDIN
An imprint of Simon & Schuster Children's Publishing Division
1230 Avenue of the Americas, New York, New York 10020
First Aladdin paperback edition January 2021
Text copyright © 2021 by Beatrice Gormley
Cover photograph copyright © 2021 by Pool/Pool (Getty Images)
Also available in an Aladdin hardcover edition.
For information about special discounts for bulk purchases,
please contact Simon & Schuster Special Sales at 1-866-506-1949
or business@simonandschuster.com.
The Simon & Schuster Speakers Bureau can bring authors to your
live event. For more information or to book an event contact the
Simon & Schuster Speakers Bureau at 1-866-248-3049
or visit our website at www.simonspeakers.com.
Designed by Michael Rosamilia
The text of this book was set in Cochin.
Manufactured in the United States of America 1220 OFF
2 4 6 8 10 9 7 5 3 1
Library of Congress Control Number 2020950133
ISBN 978-1-5344-7932-6 (hc)
ISBN 978-1-5344-7931-9 (pbk)
ISBN 978-1-5344-7933-3 (ebook)

# Contents

# Chapter 1

# A Natural Leader

Something about Joey Biden made other kids want to follow him. It wasn't the way he looked or sounded, because he was small for his age, and he stuttered. But if Joey was your friend, you could count on him. And he was a decent person, fair to everyone. And it was a lot of fun to be around him.

In Joey's neighborhood in Scranton, Pennsylvania, "fun" meant sports like football and baseball, played in the street or on a vacant lot. Since Joey was small, at first the older boys didn't want to let him play. But he kept pestering until they let him try, and he turned out to be quick and bold. "Give me the ball!" was his favorite sentence.

Of course Joey got knocked down, but he got right up again. That was what his father advised, as a general principle in life: if you get knocked down, get up.

"Fun" also included riskier games, and Joey was quick and fearless in these, too. One time, Joey and an older boy, Jimmy Kennedy, were playing near a construction site. Jimmy dared Joey to run under a moving dump truck, never imagining that Joey would take the dare. But as soon as the words were out of Jimmy's mouth, Joey ran at the truck, darted between the front and rear wheels—and came out safe on the other side.

Joey began life in Scranton, born at St. Mary's Hospital on November 20, 1942. Catherine Eugenia Finnegan (Jean) and Joseph Robinette Biden (Joe) had just gotten married the year before, and they were living with Jean's parents, Ambrose and Geraldine Finnegan. Jean and Joe named their first baby Joseph Robinette Biden Jr., after his father. They called him Joey.

Joe Biden Sr. had met Jean Finnegan in high school, when his family moved to Scranton from Wilmington, Delaware, in the 1930s. Joe was tall, handsome, and well-dressed, with smooth manners. Jean was only five feet one inch tall, but she was spirited, and she was the high school's homecoming queen. She'd grown up in Scranton, where her father was an advertising salesman for the local newspaper.

When Joey was little, Joe Sr. could support his family in fine style. He worked for his uncle Bill Sheen, who sold a waterproof sealant to the United States government for their merchant marine ships. The year before Joe was born, on December 7, 1941, the United States had entered World War II, and Sheen Armor Company's business was thriving.

Successful and generous, "Big Bill" Sheen encouraged his nephew Joe to enjoy expensive sports, like polo and riding to the hounds. Joe and his cousin Bill Sheen Jr. were like brothers. They drove new cars—Cadillacs for Bill, Buicks for Joe—and flew private planes.

The city of Scranton also prospered, while the US and its allies were fighting World War II. Scranton was a major center for coal mining and railroads. For the war effort, the US needed tremendous amounts of coal, a major energy source at that time. And freight trains were the main means of hauling coal and the steel needed to build tanks and airplanes.

Joe Biden Sr. did well at his uncle's Sheen Armor Company. They sent him to Boston to head up a branch, and the Bidens lived in a four-bedroom Colonial house in the suburbs. In 1944, Joey's sister, Valerie, was born. On weekends and holidays, Joe flew his young family back to Scranton to be with the relatives. Airplane travel was too pricey for most people in those days, but not for the Bidens.

After World War II ended in 1945, the demand for Sheen Armor Company's products dried up. However, Joe Sr. had saved enough money to open a furniture store with a friend. Unfortunately, the "friend" took the money for the store and ran off. To Jean Biden's dismay, Joe refused to hunt down his thieving partner and press charges, because he'd been a friend.

Joe Sr. had a little money left, and he went in with another partner to start a crop-dusting company. They bought an airfield on Long Island, New York, and the Bidens moved there to live. But before long that business failed too. In 1948, Jean Biden took Joey and Valerie and moved back to Scranton, to her parents. Joe gave up and followed soon afterward.

Returning to Scranton was the practical thing for the Bidens to do, but it was a big comedown for Joe Sr. to live off his in-laws. He had to take any job he could get. Jean's brothers couldn't resist rubbing it in a bit, making smart remarks about Joe's upper-class manners. Edward Blewitt Finnegan, who stuttered, sarcastically called Joe Sr. "L-L-L-Lord Joseph."

Years later Joe Biden Jr. would realize how humbling the return to Scranton had been for his father. But at the time, five-year-old Joey was perfectly happy to move in with his grandparents and his uncle Edward Blewitt. Joey and Valerie loved their uncle, who was kind to the children. They didn't care that everyone called him "Boo-Boo" because of the way he pronounced "Blewitt."

The Finnegan household also included Joey's great-aunt Gertie Blewitt, his grandmother's sister. They all lived in a two-story shingled house at 2446 North Washington Avenue, in the Green Ridge neighborhood. Green Ridge was at the end of the electric streetcar line that ran from downtown Scranton. The neighbors were mostly working-class families, of Irish descent like the Finnegans.

The families in Green Ridge were mostly Catholic, too, with immigrant roots. Their parents and grandparents had left Poland, or Ireland, or Italy and came to Pennsylvania to work in the anthracite coal mines. Priests and nuns were a familiar sight on the street, and the children always greeted them respectfully. "Good afternoon, Father. Good afternoon,

Sister." It was taken for granted that Joey would go to a Roman Catholic school, like the other children in his neighborhood, so he started school at Saint Paul's.

Joey quickly bonded with three other Green Ridge boys: Charlie Roth, Tommy Bell, and Larry Orr. They spent Saturdays, their free day, together. They could roam as far as Green Ridge Corners, where they spent their pocket money on penny candy and caps for their cap pistols, or they could explore the always interesting city dump.

A fascinating feature of Scranton for kids was the "breakers," steep piles of dirt and rock left over from coal mining. This debris was heaped up in mountains larger than the pyramids of ancient Egypt. However, the breakers were not as solid as those pyramids. And traces of coal left in the rock easily caught fire, creating slow-burning furnaces under their slopes.

One day Joey and his friends were playing around a breaker, built up by the Marvine Coal Company, in Green Ridge. Charlie bet Joey five dollars that he didn't dare to run up to the top. Maybe that seemed like a safe bet to Charlie, because the boys knew it was dangerous to climb on the loosely balanced pile. You could fall through the surface, far enough to break your neck. Or you could stumble into a hidden pit of fire.

But Joey couldn't resist a dare, especially for such big money. He charged at the mountain and kept going, as nimble as a mountain goat, until he reached the top. Inspired, Tommy followed his brave buddy up the slope.

Such a daredevil boy as Joey Biden might not seem like the type to take care of his little sister. But Joey considered Valerie, two years younger, his special charge. Not that he would stay home and babysit her—he took her along on his neighborhood adventures. As Valerie described it years later, "From the time I opened my eyes, he was there, he had his hand out and said, 'Come on, let's go.'"

Joey was Valerie's hero, and she was his loyal sidekick. He showed her how to throw a baseball and how to jump for the basketball net. He taught her to vault onto the back fender of his bicycle so she could ride everywhere with him. Years later Joey would include his much younger brothers, Jimmy and Frank, in his adventures with Valerie.

Every Sunday morning the Finnegans and Bidens went to Saint Paul's Catholic Church for Mass, like most of the neighborhood. In the afternoon, before Sunday dinner, the Finnegans, the Bidens, and assorted friends would gather at Grandpop Finnegan's house. The men sat at the kitchen table, talking sports and politics. As Joey grew older, he started to hang around the kitchen and listen, fascinated.

Grandpop and his relatives and friends argued about President Truman, a Democrat, and whether he'd been right to fire General MacArthur. They argued about General Eisenhower, a hero of World War II but unfortunately a Republican, who ran for president in 1950. They argued about how the government treated workers who were striking. They argued about local politicians, especially which ones you could trust and which ones you couldn't.

Joey didn't always understand the fine points of the men's discussion, but he did take in some key ideas. First, that politics was important. There weren't any politicians in the family, except for a former Pennsylvania state senator on Geraldine Finnegan's side. But what happened in politics had the power to change people's lives, for the better—or for the worse.

And second, Joey learned that politics could be—should be—a noble calling. In politics, as in the rest of life, your word should be your bond.

In those years, the Bidens and the Finnegans didn't know any big-time politicians. The closest Joey got to a national politician, when he was growing up, was at a Saint Patrick's Day parade. Former president Harry Truman was grand marshal of that parade, and he rode through Scranton in a convertible with the top down. The *Scranton Tribune* printed a photo of the parade showing both Truman and—in the crowd on the sidelines, fuzzy but recognizable—young Joey Biden.

Growing up, Joey learned certain values: tell the truth, say your prayers, keep your promises, be loyal to family and friends. He did *not* learn to be careful, or to stay out of trouble. One winter day, Joey and his friend Larry stood outside the Finnegan house, throwing snowballs at passing cars.

Joey was a natural athlete, with a good throwing arm. One of his snowballs went right through a truck's open window, smacking the driver in the head. When the man jumped out, furious, the boys scurried up the steps of Joey's house and in the door.

The driver ran up the steps after the boys, but Aunt Gertie fended him off. Without waiting to find out what had happened or whose fault it was, she swung her broom at the man. "Get out of here!"

Joey knew that his family would always stick by him, even when he was wrong. And he understood that he, in turn, needed to take care of his family.

☆ ☆ ☆

Besides being small for his age, Joey had a stutter, like his uncle Boo-Boo. When he was in kindergarten, his parents sent him to a speech pathologist, but that didn't seem to help. However, the stutter didn't bother Joey when he was with friends, especially playing sports. It didn't bother his friends, either. It was just part of Joey, like his blue eyes.

Saturday afternoons, Joey and his Green Ridge pals would often go to the movies at the Roosevelt Theater, usually Westerns or Tarzan movies. Inspired by the adventures on the screen, Joey and his friend Tommy would climb onto the roof of a neighborhood garage. They'd leap from that roof to the next garage, and the next, and so on until some adult yelled at them.

Another daredevil game was running on the big pipes across the Lackawanna River. The river in those days was filthy with sewage and coal-mining waste, and the boys' parents had told them to stay away from it. "But as long as we didn't fall in," Joe Biden wrote years afterward, "who would know?"

After World War II, jobs became hard to find in Scranton. Joe Biden Sr. finally decided he'd do better in Wilmington, Delaware. He'd lived in that city before, and he'd heard that Wilmington industries were doing well after the war. He took a job there cleaning boilers for Kyle Heating and Air-Conditioning. Wilmington was more than 140 miles from Scranton, but Joe Sr. drove back and forth for almost a year without complaining.

In 1952, when Joey was almost ten, his parents decided to move the whole family to Wilmington. It must have been hard for Jean Biden, who'd grown up in Scranton, to leave her town—all her family and friends and neighbors. But she didn't complain either.

# Chapter 2

# "Mr. Bu-Bu-Bu-Bu-Biden"

Joey's mother pitched the move as an exciting fresh start. Just think, she told the children, their new home was brand-new—they'd be the first people to set foot in it! Jean Biden was like that. She looked on the bright side, and she encouraged her children to look on the bright side too.

Joey Biden didn't need encouragement to be excited. Of course it was an adventure, waving goodbye to Scranton in northeastern Pennsylvania, riding all the way south past Philadelphia, and finally reaching Delaware. Joey knew that Delaware was the second-smallest state in the Union, after Rhode Island. It was also the First State—the first state to ratify the US Constitution.

Almost as soon as the Bidens crossed the state

line, they were on the outskirts of Wilmington. From the back seat of the family car, Joey, Valerie, and their little brother, Jimmy, peered out at the smoky industrial landscape. There was a steel mill, a chemical company, oil refineries.

Wilmington was the largest city in Delaware. The Bidens were moving to a section on the northern edge, called Claymont, where the steel-mill workers lived. Their new home was in Brookview Apartments, a development still under construction. Joseph Biden was still cleaning boilers for Kyle Heating and Air-Conditioning, and the family could barely afford their small apartment.

Jean Biden had decided the move was a good chance for Joey to repeat a grade. He was young and small for his class, and he'd missed some school in Scranton when he'd had his tonsils out. So Joey began third grade again at Holy Rosary, a Catholic grade school in Claymont. In his new school Joey quickly made friends and jumped into sports, his favorite activity. But he was still one of the shortest kids in his class, and that bothered him.

Joey's parents and teachers were more worried about his stutter, which held him back in schoolwork. The nuns encouraged him, telling Joey he was a good boy, a smart boy. If a classmate teased him about his stutter, the teachers defended him. So did his mother. When Joey got frustrated with his stutter, she told him how handsome he was, how smart, what a good athlete. "You've got so much to say, honey, that your brain gets ahead of you."

In spite of challenges with schoolwork, Joey began to dream big about where he wanted to go to high school. His choice was Archmere Academy, a college preparatory school close by in Claymont. Joey could see his dream school, a marble mansion, from his upstairs bedroom window. And when he played football in the Catholic Youth Organization, he and his team entered Archmere's wrought-iron gates and practiced on the school's spacious grounds. Joey loved to imagine his future self in high school, a star athlete at Archmere Academy.

Meanwhile, Joey was comfortable with the nuns— the teaching sisters—at Holy Rosary. Along with the usual reading and writing and math, they taught values: fairness, helpfulness, honesty, courage. They taught the children that when a bully was picking on somebody, the noble thing to do was to stand up to the bully.

The nuns' values were the same as the ones that

Joey's mother and father taught their children around the kitchen table. Joseph and Jean Biden could not stand meanness, and they could not stand people who used their power to tyrannize others. Another Biden principle: if you make a promise, keep it—for your own honor and for your family's. "My word as a Biden" was a solemn oath.

One of Joey's favorite teachers was Sister Lawrence Joseph, who played baseball with the kids at recess. Lifting the long skirts of her habit, she ran the bases. Like a good coach, she encouraged Joey not to worry about his size. "You know, my brother was small too, Joey, but he was a really good athlete."

In 1955 the Bidens moved from the apartment in Claymont to a new split-level house in Mayfield, closer to downtown Wilmington. In Mayfield, most of the families were Protestant, and most of the fathers were college-educated. They worked for DuPont Chemical—a successful and growing corporation—as chemists, lawyers, or accountants.

Later in life, Joe Biden reflected that his father must have felt out of place in this neighborhood. Joseph Biden was now the manager of a Chevrolet dealership. Selling cars was a better job than cleaning boilers, but not a professional job like the other fathers had. However, Joseph took pride in dressing well, and he went off to work every day wearing a suit and tie, his shoes shined, his fingernails manicured.

Sometimes, looking into his father's closet, Joey wondered about the black equestrian boots and the polo stick, gear for expensive sports that Joseph Biden would never play again. He gazed at pictures of the horses that his father used to keep on his uncle's estate on Long Island. Joey sensed a big disconnect there, but his father never talked about his high-flying early life.

Living in Mayfield, Joey attended Saint Helena's, another Catholic school. Like many of the other boys, Joey admired the priests, and once he even asked his mother if he could go to a training school to become a priest. Jean Biden put him off, telling her son that he was too young to make such a decision. Another ambition popped up around the same time: Joey wrote in a paper for school that when he grew up, he wanted to be president of the United States. Of course, as he remarked years later, so did a lot of other twelve-year-olds.

Meanwhile, Joey was more and more aware that his stutter was holding him back. Not in sports, where he didn't need to talk much, and not with his friends, where he was relaxed. Besides, his friends at Saint Helena's were being raised, as he was, to be respectful. They would never tease a person about their physical disability or their unlucky circumstances in life.

But with adults Joey didn't know well, or when he felt as if he were onstage, he tensed up and stuttered. He had a paper route in Mayfield, and every Saturday he had to go around and collect subscription money from his customers. To avoid stumbling over words, he rehearsed each conversation. Since his next-door neighbor, Mr. Walsh, was a Yankees fan, Joey would check the baseball box scores before he knocked on the door. He'd be ready to say, "D'ja see Mantle hit two homers yesterday?"

At school, the most unnerving times were when Joey had to recite or read aloud. He prepared himself for this even more intensely. Luckily for him, the students were seated in rows alphabetically by last name. Since young Biden was always in the first row, he could figure out which passages in the textbook he might have to read aloud. He memorized these passages and practiced a rhythm of speaking that avoided tripping up his tongue.

One day Joey had prepared himself to read, "Sir

Walter Raleigh was a gentleman. He took off his cloak and laid it over the mud so the lady would not dirty her shoes." Sure enough, the teacher called on him to read that passage.

Joey started off confidently, but then the teacher interrupted him in the middle of the first sentence, throwing him off his stride. She asked him to repeat one of the words. Joey started again, but his rhythm was broken. He began to stutter.

The teacher imitated his speech: "Mr. Bu-Bu-Bu-Bu-Biden . . ."

Joey couldn't believe it. Up until now, his teachers had tried to help him overcome his stutter. But this nun was actually making fun of his disability. In front of the whole class.

"I could feel a white heat come up through my legs and the back of my neck," Joe Biden wrote years later. "It was pure rage. I got up from my desk and walked out of the classroom, right past the nun." He stalked out of the school and kept walking for two miles, all the way home.

Saint Helena's telephoned Jean Biden to let her know that Joey had left the school, but not why. So Joey's mother was waiting for him, shocked and angry—at her son. After ordering Joey into the car along with his littlest brother, Frankie, she drove back toward the school. "Joey," she asked grimly, "what happened?"

"Mom, she made fun of me," he answered. "She called me 'Mr. Bu-Bu-Bu-Bu-Biden.'"

Jean Biden deeply respected the Catholic Church and its nuns and priests, and she brought her children up to have the same respect. But this day she marched into the school, sat Joey down outside the principal's office with toddler Frankie on his lap, marched into the office, and demanded to see Joey's teacher.

The teacher, dressed in her usual nun's habit and bonnet, was called to the office. At first, she tried to deny that she'd said anything out of line. But Joey's mother insisted on a straight answer: *Had* she mocked Joey's stutter?

"Yes, Mrs. Biden," said the nun defensively. "I was making a point."

At that, Joe Biden wrote later, "I could see my mother pull herself up to her full height, five foot one." Jean Biden stepped up to the nun and said, "If you ever speak to my son like that again, I'll come back and rip that bonnet off your head. Do you understand me?"

Although Wilmington was several hours' drive from the Bidens' old home in Scranton, the distance didn't keep them away from Grandpop Finnegan's house in Green Ridge. Joe and Jean Biden, with Joey, Valerie, Jimmy, and eventually baby Frankie, drove up to Scranton for Thanksgiving, for Christmas, for birthdays, for summer vacations. Joey's old neighborhood pals saw him so often that some of them didn't realize he'd moved away.

And the boys would still go off together for the same kinds of fun. One summer Sunday in Scranton, when Joey and Charlie, Tommy, and Larry were twelve or thirteen, the boys started a water balloon fight. They were up on a ledge, with the road down below.

Spotting a young man driving by in an open convertible, his arm around his girlfriend, Joey shouted, "Let 'em have it!" The first balloon hit the hood of the car. The second one landed right in the front seat, next to the girl.

The driver jumped out of the car, wet and furious, and took off after the boys. "This guy would not give up," said Larry Orr years later. The driver chased them all the way to the next town, Dunmore. The boys managed to shake him, finally, by hiding behind tombstones in a cemetery.

One of the first and most lasting values Joey learned, growing up, was family loyalty. He was supposed to watch out for his sister and brothers, and they were supposed to watch out for him. "You're closer to one another than you are to your dad and me," his mother told them. In a tough choice, family came first.

A tough choice for Joey came when he had the job of keeping order on the school bus. Joey was proud of being chosen for safety patrol, and of wearing his blue badge. But one day it was Val, as he called his sister, who misbehaved on the bus. He was supposed to report kids who misbehaved—but turn in his own sister? Joey asked his father what he should do.

"She's your sister, Joey."

Joey understood. To be loyal to his sister, he couldn't report her. But if he couldn't do his job on safety patrol, he would have to resign. The next day, he gave up his blue badge.

By the time Joey was in the eighth grade, he was well aware that his family's money was tight. If he wore a hole in the bottom of his shoe, he might have to put a piece of cardboard inside until his father's next payday. When he was invited to a dance, he had to scrape together an outfit from his father's clothes.

Joseph Biden's dress shirt was much too big for Joey, so his mother turned the cuffs back and fastened them like French cuffs. Only, she couldn't find his father's cuff links. When she came back with nuts and bolts instead, Joey was horrified. "I am not going to wear this. The kids will make fun of me."

Calmly fastening the cuffs with the hardware, Jean Biden told her son, "If anybody says anything to you about these nuts and bolts, you just look them right in the eye and say, 'Don't you have a pair of these?'"

At the dance, it turned out that Joey was right. While he was pouring himself a drink at the punch bowl, a boy grabbed his arm and exclaimed, "Look at Biden! Nuts and bolts!"

But Jean Biden was right too. Heeding her advice, Joey stared at the other boy. "Don't you have a pair of these?"

The confidence in Joey's voice must have shaken the other boy. There was a silence, while the group waited to see what he would answer. Finally he seemed to decide that nuts-and-bolts cuff links must be the latest fad. "Yeah," he said. "I got a pair of these."

As Joe progressed through the seventh and eighth grades at Saint Helena's, he fixed his sights more than ever on Archmere Academy. But the tuition at Archmere was $300 a year. His father tried to get Joe to consider a less expensive Catholic high school, or even the public high school.

Joe understood that his family couldn't afford to pay the tuition, but that didn't change his determination to go to Archmere. There had to be another way. After passing the Archmere entrance examination, he applied for a work-study program. Joe would do work for the school, and in exchange, his tuition fees would be waived.

So the summer before his freshman year of high school, Joe worked on the Archmere grounds crew. Every day, from eight in the morning until four in the afternoon, he was one of a crew of about ten. The groundskeeper was a hoarse-voiced, bad-tempered fellow named Dominic, always growling complaints about the headmaster, Father Justin Diny.

First Joe spent days weeding the formal gardens around the Archmere mansion. Next, he washed every window in the mansion itself, swabbing the glass with a rag soaked in vinegar and water, and drying it with newspaper. And then he painted the wrought-iron fence that surrounded the estate.

Tactfully, Archmere didn't embarrass the work-study boys by making them work during the school year. That first morning in September, Joe dressed in the school uniform of jacket and tie, and packed his new fountain pen, pencils, and notebooks. The school bus carried him between the stone pillars at the entrance, where he noted the fresh black paint on the wrought-iron gates. Up at the mansion, he silently admired the gleaming windows.

Just inside the mansion was a foyer with marble pillars and a retractable stained-glass ceiling. Joe Biden, now a student at Archmere Academy, belonged in this magnificent place. With determination and a lot of hard work, he had made this dream come true.

# Chapter 3

# "Ask What You Can Do for Your Country"

Joe Biden was thrilled to be attending Archmere. But he still wished he weren't so short. At age fourteen, he was five foot one and barely weighed one hundred pounds. Only one boy in his class was smaller.

Worse, Joe's stutter was more of a problem for him than ever. Archmere, a college preparatory school, expected its students to learn public speaking. It was one thing to memorize a paragraph to read aloud, as Joe had at Saint Helena's. It was quite another to stand in front of 250 boys and deliver a five-minute speech. But that was a requirement at Archmere—every student had to take a turn giving a presentation at morning assembly.

Because of his stutter, Joe was excused from the speech requirement the first year. This made life easier for him in a way, but he knew that his fellow students all understood why he was the only boy to be excused. And these college prep boys were less kind and more competitive than his friends in grade school.

They nicknamed him "Joe Impedimenta," using a word they'd learned in Latin class. They also called him "Dash," meaning that he spoke like Morse code, *dot-dot-dash*. "They looked at me like I was stupid," Joe Biden wrote later.

The teasing shamed Joe and filled him with rage. And he realized what a threat the stutter was to his ambitions. He intended to do great things with his life, but the stutter loomed as an *impediment*, a roadblock, on the way to achieving his aims.

Just look at Uncle Boo-Boo, who'd come from Scranton to live with the Bidens in Wilmington. Edward Blewitt Finnegan was a smart man, a college graduate who'd wanted to become a doctor. But because of his stutter, he was selling mattresses for a living.

As much as Joe loved Uncle Boo-Boo, he was afraid of ending up like him. Life had dealt both of them an unfair blow, saddling them with a stutter. But as Joseph Biden advised his children, "If you get knocked down, get up."

So Joe worked hard at overcoming his impediment. He memorized long passages and practiced speaking in front of his bedroom mirror. Watching closely, he tried to keep his jaw muscles from clenching. If he saw his face tightening up, he'd pause, smile, try to relax his facial muscles, and then go on.

Joe was willing to try anything that might help him conquer his stutter. He'd heard the story of Demosthenes, a famous orator of ancient Greece. Demosthenes, too, had grown up with a bad stutter. He'd conquered it by practicing speeches on the seashore, with pebbles in his mouth.

Mayfield wasn't near the ocean and its pebbles, but a neighbor of the Bidens happened to have a pebbled path. Helping himself to a handful, Joe put them in his mouth and tried to project his voice off a brick wall. "I nearly swallowed half the pebbles," he wrote later. And it didn't help his stutter.

In spite of his struggles, or maybe because of them, Archmere was the right place for Joe Biden. In his first two years, he grew a whole foot. He'd been a fierce athlete even when he was short, but with his new size he became one of the best players on the football team, the Archers. He was fast, and he was amazingly good at catching a football. His team members gave him a new and much better nickname, "Hands," for his skill at catching passes.

Joe also had something maybe even more valuable than size or skill: a winning attitude. "He always had confidence, or made everybody believe he had confidence," said his teammate Tom Lewis. "He'd never shy from a confrontation."

Joe continued to work on his stutter, encouraged by his teachers and especially by his mother, his biggest booster. He also had the sympathy of Uncle Boo-Boo, who understood exactly how Joe felt. But Joe could see that his uncle used his stutter as a crutch, an excuse for never doing much with his life.

When Joe was a sophomore at Archmere, he finally stood up in front of morning assembly and gave the required five-minute speech. "No excuses, no exemptions, just like everybody else," he wrote proudly years afterward.

Now that his stutter was under control, Joe discovered that he *liked* to talk. In fact, he had a natural "gift of gab," as the Irish expression goes. And he had a lot he wanted to talk about.

Joe was earning Bs at Archmere and was learning a great deal, especially in politics and history. He could talk and talk about these subjects, so much that his classmates teased him.

Joe's interest in politics went back to the lively discussions around Grandpop Finnegan's kitchen table in Scranton. And in the Biden household in Wilmington, Joe's father expected his children to be informed about public affairs. At dinner table discussions, Joseph often brought up big topics: equality, justice, the horrors of the Holocaust in Nazi Germany.

Uncle Boo-Boo made Joe read the *New York Times* editorial page, and he argued politics with Joe and his friends. One time he drove Joe and Val to Washington, DC, to see the Capitol, where the United States Congress met. Joe's uncle even introduced them to an actual US senator, Everett Dirksen of Illinois.

In Joe's last two years at Archmere, his social life blossomed. Outgoing and friendly, he was popular with girls, and now he didn't have to worry about stuttering when he asked them out. He and his friends went to high school dances at the DuPont Country Club and met each other at the Charcoal Pit for hamburgers and jukebox music. His girlfriend at that time was Maureen Masterson, a few years younger than Joe. Maureen attended Ursuline Academy, a Catholic girls' school, where Valerie Biden was her best friend.

More than ever, Joe was a natural leader. Others were drawn to him by his confidence and his upbeat attitude. His leadership style was to make everyone feel included, especially those who might be left out. He'd notice a younger boy who was being teased and deliberately invite him to come along with Joe and his friends.

For Joe's senior year at Archmere, 1960–61, the football team had a new coach, John Walsh. The Archmere Archers had been winning less than one game per year for the last twelve years. As Walsh put his new team through practice sessions, he chose Joe Biden and his teammate Mike Fay as halfbacks.

The coach knew that Joe wanted very much to be team captain, but he tapped Mike instead. However, the coach was impressed with Joe's reaction: he accepted the coach's decision, and he didn't sulk. He just kept on playing his best for the team.

Shaped into a tightly bonded unit by Coach Walsh, the Archers began the season by winning their first game. Then they won their second game, and their third, and so on through the season. Halfback Joe Biden was the leading scorer. Whatever the situation on the field, he had a detailed idea of how he could make a touchdown. And his favorite four words were still, "Give me the ball."

# **Racial Segregation**

After Reconstruction ended in 1877, Southern states began to pass laws against racial integration. The mingling of Black people with white people—in schools, on trains and streetcars, in theaters, in restaurants, on beaches—was forbidden. In 1896 these laws were challenged in the courts. But the Supreme Court ruled that separating Black people and white people in public places was legal, as long as the accommodations for each race were equal. This ruling officially began the "Jim Crow" period, in which segregation was the law across the South.

However, the "equal" part of the Supreme Court's ruling was never enforced. The separate restrooms, drinking fountains, and especially the schools for Blacks were inferior or even nonexistent. In 1954 the Supreme Court ruled that separating Black children and white children in the public schools was unconstitutional, and therefore illegal.

But many school systems, especially in the South, were very slow to begin desegregating. And the federal government, with Dwight D. Eisenhower as president, did not enforce the court's ruling. Schools remained segregated, and so did public transportation. On buses, for instance, Black passengers were expected to sit in the back, in the "colored" section.

In the North, there might not have been laws *requiring* segregation by race, but restaurants and hotels often refused to allow Black customers. Real-estate agents in many areas would not sell property or rent homes to Blacks, and banks would not offer them mortgages. So Black people were forced to live only in certain neighborhoods, and their children went to schools only in those districts. The result was not only segregated housing but also segregated schools.

During the early 1960s, racial segregation was the unwritten rule in Wilmington. Many white high school students were unaware of the racial barriers. But Joe noticed, and the unfairness bothered him. One time, as Mike Fay remembered later, the Archmere football team went to the Charcoal Pit as usual. Frank Hutchins, the only Black student at Archmere, was in the group.

As the hungry team poured into the dining room,

an employee stopped Frank. Frank couldn't come in with the rest of the boys, he was told. If he wanted to buy a hamburger, he'd have to go to the take-out window.

Seeing Frank shut out, Joe, Mike, and the rest of the football team all had the same reaction. Without discussing the problem, they got up and left the diner.

Joe was elected class president for both his junior and senior years at Archmere. Valerie, Joe's second-biggest booster after their mother, handed out flyers for his campaigns. Joe would have run for student body president, but Father Diny, the headmaster, discouraged the idea. Joe had built up a number of demerits, and Father Diny pointed out that a leader ought to be a role model too.

However, at Joe's graduation from Archmere in June 1961, it was his charge as class president to give the class welcome. He stepped onto the stage in front of his classmates' friends and families and performed this duty perfectly. "Without a single stammer," he wrote later in his memoir.

Back in November 1960, during the first semester of Joe Biden's senior year at Archmere Academy, Senator

John F. Kennedy had been elected president of the United States. Since president-elect Kennedy was from a Catholic family, many Catholic Americans— including the Bidens and the Finnegans—were overjoyed. The United States at that time was mainly a Protestant country, with a long-standing bias against Catholics.

President Kennedy was also younger than any other candidate ever elected president of the US. He was forty-three, quite a contrast with outgoing President Dwight Eisenhower, age seventy. In January 1961, young people across the country were inspired by President Kennedy's inaugural address, especially these words: "Ask not what your country can do for you. Ask what you can do for your country."

This appeal spoke to Joe, drawing him toward a career in public service. His friend Dave Walsh later remembered his father asking Joe what he wanted to do in life. "Mr. Walsh," Joe answered, "I want to be president of the United States." To both Dave and his father, it seemed perfectly possible. Such a determined, talented, hardworking boy as Joe Biden might indeed grow up to become the leader of the free world.

Typical of Joe, he wasn't content with having a dream. To reach his goal, he needed a plan. How did somebody like him, without any money or big connections, go about becoming a politician? Joe went to the Archmere library and looked up senators and congressmen in the *Congressional Directory*. Many of them, he discovered, had started out as lawyers.

That made sense, because trial lawyers got up in court and spoke to judges and juries. They persuaded their listeners by means of their knowledge and public speaking skills. Politicians would need those same skills to connect with voters, as well as with other policy makers. Joe, having mastered his disability, could aim to become a lawyer.

That fall Joe began college life at the University of Delaware, where he majored in political science and history. Those studies would prepare him to go to law school after college, and the law degree would prepare him for politics. These were the steps in his master plan for his life.

Of course, the catch was that Joe would have to actually study. There were so many social events at Delaware, and Joe loved getting together with other people. He went to dozens of dances and fraternity parties, in spite of the fact that he didn't drink alcohol or smoke. He didn't even belong to a fraternity.

Joe had seen alcohol abuse in his own family,

especially with Uncle Boo-Boo. He didn't admire the way his uncle would drink and then talk big about what he could have accomplished in life. Joe didn't want to take a chance on becoming an alcoholic himself.

Besides, Joe could have a great time at parties without drinking. As his sister, Valerie, explained later, "Joe would do wild and crazy things but he was always sober. You couldn't blame it [on] because he had too much to drink." Joe was always the designated driver in his group of friends.

He always had a car to drive too, which wasn't true of many students. By this time Joseph Biden owned his own car dealership, and he would let Joe borrow a car from the lot on weekends. Joe dated a lot of girls, often on double dates with Valerie and a friend of his. Outgoing, good-looking, and nicely dressed, Joe was elected president of his freshman class at the University of Delaware.

During the summer after his freshman year, 1962, Joe worked as a lifeguard at a public swimming pool. The pool was next to a public housing project, Prices Run, in a mostly Black neighborhood, and Joe was the only white lifeguard. One day a gang member started fooling around in the pool, bouncing on the high board. Blowing his whistle, Joe sarcastically called him "Esther Williams" (a famous movie swim star). Joe ordered the youth out of the pool and escorted him to the parking lot.

Fortunately, Joe realized that the incident could turn nasty, and he quickly got his temper under control. He apologized for insulting the macho gang member by calling him a woman's name. At the same time, Joe pointed out, everyone had to follow the pool rules.

Getting to know the other lifeguards at the pool was an education for Joe. He'd been aware that movie theaters in Wilmington were segregated by race, and he'd taken part in a couple of marches to desegregate them. In high school, Joe had walked out of the Charcoal Pit when they'd treated his Black teammate, Frank, unfairly. But now, for the first time, he was the only white guy in a group of Black men his own age.

As Joe worked with his fellow lifeguards, chatted with them, and played basketball with them, he felt almost like an exchange student in a foreign country. His new friends were college students, like him, but they attended Black colleges. He was the only white guy they knew, and they curiously asked him questions about his way of life.

In turn, Joe heard about how their lives were

blighted by a constant stream of insults and injuries. They could be beaten up, for instance, for using the public drinking fountain in a white neighborhood. When they went to the movies, they had to sit in the "colored" section. Even though Joe had known about the movie theaters being segregated, it wasn't until now that he truly saw how much it hurt his Black friends to be treated like second-class citizens.

Joe's lifeguarding experience helped him understand how much was at stake in the ongoing civil rights struggle. The next year, in May 1963, Joe and other Americans around the country watched shocking scenes on the TV news. During a civil rights march in Birmingham, Alabama, police chief Bull Connor turned fire hoses and attack dogs on the young marchers. And Joe read Dr. Martin Luther King Jr.'s "Letter from Birmingham Jail," a powerful explanation of why the civil rights marches were necessary.

That same year, 1963, Joe took a trip to Washington, DC. He was especially eager to revisit the Capitol Building, where the US Congress—the House of Representatives and the Senate—met. This was where he planned to be someday, to do his part in national politics. Joe's hero President Kennedy had first run for the office of senator from Massachusetts, and then, as senator, he had run for the highest office in the land.

At the massive white-domed building on Capitol Hill, Joe stepped into the Senate Chamber in the north wing. The Senate was not in session at the moment, and Joe had a chance to stare around the empty room. Along one wall, decorated with dark red marble pilasters, was the marble rostrum, and the chair where the presiding officer sat. Semicircular rows of desks, one desk for each of the hundred senators, faced the rostrum. All around the room on the second floor, a visitor's gallery overlooked the scene.

This was the center of power. As Joe sank into the presiding officer's chair, the thought gave him goose bumps. Here, senators hammered out laws that changed Americans' lives for the better—or for the worse.

Joe's ambitious musings were interrupted by the hand of a uniformed security guard on his back. Unescorted visitors, the man informed him, were not allowed in the Senate Chamber. The guard marched Joe down to a room in the basement of the Capitol. He questioned him severely before letting the starstruck young man go.

As a freshman at the University of Delaware, Joe had gone out for football again. He loved playing the game so much that he'd toyed with the idea of a pro football career. But after Joe's first-semester grades came out, his parents told him he had to drop football.

Joseph Biden was especially worried that Joe was letting his grades slide. Joe Sr. was set on his oldest son becoming the first Biden to graduate from college. "Remember, Joey, you gotta be a college man," he urged him. "They can never take your degree from you."

So Joe gave up football after freshman year, but still he was only skating along on C grades. He was having too much fun. He was put on probation for one of his wilder stunts, spraying an RA (resident assistant) with a fire extinguisher.

And Joe spent many hours hanging around the dormitory lounge when he should have been studying instead. He argued with his friends about civil rights, about President Kennedy's policy toward Cuba, about their own futures. Joe's friend Fred Sears, who had also gone from Archmere Academy to the University of Delaware, assumed that Joe didn't have a chance of getting into law school.

But at the beginning of his junior year, Joe woke up to an inconvenient fact. There was a direct connection between his grades and the next step in his master plan: becoming a lawyer. He had to improve his grade average. Fast.

# Chapter 4

# Lovestruck and
# Law School

Finally getting serious about his college grades, Joe Biden went to a political science professor at the University of Delaware for advice. The professor told him bluntly that he had no chance of getting into law school unless he could achieve an *excellent* academic record for his last year and a half. So Joe moved off campus, away from the lively social life. After signing up for challenging courses, he studied all the time.

Not surprisingly, his grades shot up. By spring break in 1964, Joe felt confident enough about his progress to think about going out for football again. He even allowed himself to take a vacation in Florida.

Like throngs of other college students, Joe and his friend Fred Sears piled into a classmate's car and headed for Fort Lauderdale, over a thousand miles away. But when they reached Fort Lauderdale, the beach scene wasn't as much fun as Joe and Fred had hoped. Too many male students, they thought, and not nearly enough females.

The two friends learned that a round-trip plane ride to Nassau, a resort town in the Bahamas, was only twenty-eight dollars. Without thinking it over much, they bought tickets and hopped on the plane. Joe and Fred had no money for a hotel. But they quickly found other college guys with a Nassau apartment and paid them a few dollars to sleep on their floor.

Then Joe and Fred headed for the public beach. A chain-link fence divided it from a private beach belonging to an expensive hotel. And the private beach was full of attractive young women.

On the fence separating Joe and Fred from the young women, they noticed some beach towels with the hotel's logo. They grabbed the towels, wrapped them around their waists, and strolled in the front door of the hotel as if they belonged there. No one stopped them, so they walked on through the hotel to the private beach.

There Joe spotted a girl so gorgeous that he knew he had to meet her. Fred saw her too, but Joe, quicker and more determined, got to her lounge chair first. "Hi, I'm Joe Biden."

She looked up at the guy with the dazzling smile and said, "Hi, Joe. I'm Neilia Hunter."

Joe and Neilia fell madly in love. They spent the next four days together, talking and talking. She found out that he intended to become a politician and do great things for the country. He found out that she understood a lot about politics.

Neilia lived in Skaneateles, a town in the Finger Lakes district of upstate New York. She was a senior at Syracuse University, just north of Skaneateles. She loved working with kids, and she was going to start teaching next fall.

By the time Joe joined Fred on the plane back to Fort Lauderdale, Joe was sure that he would marry Neilia. He'd planned exactly how he would do it: He would study hard during his senior year, in order to get into Syracuse University's law school after graduation. Meanwhile, starting the following weekend, he'd drive from Wilmington to Syracuse and spend every spare moment each weekend with Neilia.

The next person Joe told about Neilia was his sister, Valerie, then a freshman at the University of

Delaware. Back in Wilmington, he burst into the Bidens' house and ran up the stairs yelling, "Val!"

Valerie was talking to a friend on the phone, but she hung up. Joe blurted out, "I met the girl I'm going to marry!" Valerie had double-dated with her brother since high school days, and she knew immediately that this new girlfriend was something different.

Neilia, back in her hometown of Skaneateles, was a *little* more cautious when she called her college roommate, Bobbie. But she couldn't hide her excitement about this amazing guy, Joe Biden. "Do you know what he's going to be? He's going to be a senator by age thirty and president of the United States!" As Bobbie could tell, Neilia was "completely over the moon" about Joe.

The first weekend, Joe showed up at Neilia's house driving a flashy turquoise convertible from his father's used-car lot. Bobbie and the rest of their friends were impressed, with Joe as well as the car. Over the coming months, Neilia's parents got to know Joe. They were impressed too, although Neilia's father was uneasy about the fact that Joe was Catholic.

When Joe took Neilia to Wilmington to meet his family, the Bidens threw a big barbecue, inviting all their friends. Neilia fit in as if she belonged, and everyone, especially Val, loved her. Valerie was planning to be a teacher, like Neilia, and they had a lot in common.

Meanwhile, with Joe's life goals clearer than ever, football didn't seem so important. He informed his football coach that he was not going to try out for the varsity team his senior year. Instead Joe studied even harder.

In spite of spending every weekend with Neilia, driving back and forth from Wilmington to Syracuse, 270 miles each way, he did pull his grades up. At the end of the spring semester in 1965, Joe graduated from the University of Delaware with a BA degree in history and political science. And the Syracuse University law school, noting his improved grade average, his decent score on the Law School Admission Test, and the letters of recommendation from his professors, admitted Joseph R. Biden Jr. He would begin in September.

His next problem was how to pay for law school, which was going to cost $3,000 more than he had saved. Joe's parents couldn't pay the whole cost; they were still supporting Valerie, Jimmy, and Frank. But Joe received scholarships to make up the rest of the tuition fees. To pay for room and board, he got a job at Syracuse University as a resident advisor, living in a dormitory with undergraduate students.

At law school, Joe quickly took to the social life. He spent most of his free time with Neilia, as he'd planned, and they gathered a group of friends around them. One of the first classmates Joe met, who became a close friend, was Jack Owens.

Jack wasn't dating anyone in particular, and Joe and Neilia agreed that Jack would be the perfect match for Valerie Biden. They wanted everyone, especially these two special people, to be as happy as they were. However, when they managed to lure Valerie up from the University of Delaware to meet Jack, the two could hardly stand each other, even for one evening. The Valerie-Jack match would have to wait almost ten more years.

Joe now felt wistful about missing out on varsity football during his senior year of college. So at Syracuse, he used his leadership skills to organize an intramural team of law school students. He quarterbacked them, his teammates kidded him, as if they were in the Olympics.

By now Joe Biden had his stuttering problem well under control, although it would be there in the background for the rest of his life. He was always mindful of his ambition to become a trial lawyer and then a politician. He practiced public speaking every chance he got, including to high school classes.

During this time he learned something very important about public speaking. When he knew what he wanted to say, he could look out at the audience rather than down at his notes. And seeing the audience's reactions, he could adjust his remarks to them. Connecting with his listeners made him a better speaker, and he loved it. He could imagine how well he'd use these skills to convince a trial jury.

Joe Biden's friends teased him about enjoying the sound of his own voice, calling him "Mr. Soapbox." On one occasion, they presented him with an actual wooden soapbox, the traditional platform for a street-corner orator. An old pair of his sneakers was fastened on top of it.

Joe was pleased with himself, but he also wanted to share his hard-won skill in speaking fluently. In the dormitory where he lived as a resident advisor, he noticed a freshman who had a severe stutter. Taking the young man under his wing, Joe showed him how to practice speaking in front of a mirror. And to build up his confidence, Joe brought him along to Neilia's house, including him in gatherings of their friends.

With all these activities, the one thing Joe *didn't* do was study. The coursework bored him. He viewed law school as just something to get through, a necessary step in his life plan. "I was a dangerous combination of arrogant and sloppy," he admitted later in his memoir, *Promises to Keep*. He skipped classes; if he went to the law school library, he spent more time chatting with other students than poring over law books.

Everyone Joe Biden met was impressed with his confidence. Two of his classmates later remembered a time when a professor called on Joe to discuss a case. Joe hadn't read the case, but he started talking anyway.

As he went on and on in convincing detail, the other students began to catch on and laugh. Joe was making the whole case up, on the spot, and discussing this imaginary case. When he sat down, the class burst out applauding.

Amazingly, Joe managed to get decent grades at the end of the first semester. Other students were envious of Joe's ability to slide by. "You knew Joe was different," said one classmate, Bill Kissell. If he'd studied only as much as Joe, Bill was sure he'd have flunked out. "He had other projects," Bill added wryly, "and Neilia was clearly one of them."

And Joe was Neilia's project. Joe had never met anyone, outside of his own family, who believed in him so absolutely. They planned their life together, agreeing on almost everything.

First they would get married. While Neilia continued teaching, Joe would finish law school. Then he would practice law as a trial lawyer and start his own law firm. He would run for public office, win his elections, and work to make people's lives better.

## Civil Rights, Voting Rights

President John F. Kennedy proposed a civil rights bill, prohibiting racial discrimination, in 1963, but a Southern minority in the Senate filibustered that bill to death. After Kennedy was assassinated in November, the new president, Lyndon Johnson, was determined to steer the Civil Rights Act of 1964 through Congress. The bill quickly passed the House of Representatives, but again the "Southern bloc" in the Senate launched a filibuster that lasted from April to June.

Finally Senator Hubert Humphrey, the majority whip, assembled enough votes to cut off the filibuster. The Senate passed the bill, and President Johnson signed the Civil Rights Act of

1964 into law. Now the federal government had the power to prevent segregation in schools, on buses, and in restaurants. The act also included a voting rights section, but unfortunately, it was too weak to do much good.

So one of the worst restrictions on African Americans in the South remained: they were not allowed to vote. Some states charged Black citizens (but not whites) a poll tax—a fee for voting—that they knew most Blacks could not afford. Some required Black citizens (but not whites) to pass a difficult "literacy test"—for instance, reading aloud a long passage filled with legal jargon from the state constitution. In other places, Black people were threatened with violence if they tried to register to vote.

During the Freedom Summer of 1964, civil rights workers led a huge voter registration drive in Mississippi. It did not succeed in its goal— three of the civil rights volunteers were murdered, and most Black citizens did not even try to register. But the civil rights movement forged on. Early in 1965, Dr. Martin Luther King Jr. led several demonstrations in Selma, Alabama.

On Bloody Sunday, March 7, marchers led

by John Lewis were attacked near Selma, at the Edmund Pettus Bridge, by state troopers on horseback with whips and tear gas. One man was killed, and Lewis and many other people were badly injured. Americans who watched the violent scenes on TV were horrified, and the civil rights demonstrators gained much sympathy for their cause. In August, Congress passed the Voting Rights Act of 1965, prohibiting any state voting law that discriminated against a racial group.

Joe and Neilia also talked about the kind of home they envisioned: a roomy Tudor-style house on a spacious lot with big trees. They both wanted lots of children. And of course they would welcome friends and family to their home.

There was one exception to Joe's record for sliding by that first year. In fact, he did something careless that would come back to haunt him in the future. Writing a paper for a technical writing course, he used some text from the *Fordham Law Review* without giving proper credit. As Joe told it later, he didn't even know how to cite a source—because he'd cut the class in which citation was explained.

His professors took this mistake very seriously, and Joe had to appear before a faculty meeting. The professors and deans decided that Mr. Biden hadn't cheated on purpose, but the incident went on his record. He received an F in the course, and he would have to take it over again in order to get his law degree.

Toward the end of the first year, with final exams looming, Joe realized that he was in serious trouble again. He had exactly ten days to cram a year's worth of coursework into his head. Neilia came to the rescue, using her teaching skills to draw up study sheets for him. Joe, for the first time in his life, began drinking coffee to stay awake all night. In the end, he managed to avoid flunking out.

So he survived his first year of law school. That summer, he and Neilia were married. Joe was touched that her Protestant, Republican father had come to accept Neilia's marrying a Catholic — and a Democrat, to boot. On August 27, 1966, Neilia and Joe were married in a Catholic church in Skaneateles. The Hunters hosted a big reception at the country club.

The wedding was a joyous celebration with all

of Joe's family, as well as friends from Scranton, Wilmington, Archmere Academy, the University of Delaware, and law school. Two of Joe's buddies from the Scranton days, Larry Orr and Charlie Roth, were his ushers.

The newlyweds moved into a small apartment in Syracuse, in a neighborhood of modest houses. Neilia could walk to nearby Bellevue, the school where she taught eighth grade. The Bidens opened their home to their old friends, including Neilia's former roommate, Bobbie, and her husband, Dan Greene. And they started making new friends with the neighbors.

Joe still had two years of law school to complete, but he took time from studying to organize the local young people for sports: stickball, football, or whatever they could play on the streets. Driving around the neighborhood in his light green sports car, a '67 Corvette, Joe would round up kids for a game. He and Neilia, the beautiful, outgoing local teacher, were a glamorous couple in the neighborhood.

Both Neilia and Joe loved having kids around. They often invited girls and boys over for dinner. They let them play with their new dog, a German shepherd named Senator. One boy, Kevin Coyne, formed a special attachment with the Bidens. Kevin had a speech impediment, and certain older boys teased him about it. Once, when Joe happened to overhear those boys tormenting Kevin, he jumped over the fence and scolded them fiercely.

"He scared the daylights out of them," Kevin remembered with satisfaction. Kevin became a helpful young friend to the Bidens, walking Senator for them and giving them tips on where to shop.

Neilia likewise befriended a young girl, Pat Cowin, in her eighth-grade class at Bellevue. Pat's own mother was often ill and unable to take care of her, but Neilia gave Pat some of the special attention she longed for.

To supplement Neilia's small teaching salary, Joe took several odd jobs during his summers. He worked at a marina on Skaneateles Lake, as a hotel night clerk, and for the Schaefer Beer company.

In the spring of 1968, Joe Biden received his law degree. He was only seventy-eighth in a class of eighty-five, but he'd made a deep impression on many of his teachers and fellow students. James Weeks, the technical writing professor who had given Biden an F the first time around, described his former student as "far from distinguished scholastically." However, he added, "He knows what he is doing and appears to possess good judgment and a highly developed sense of responsibility."

# Chapter 5

# The Importance of Politics

Now that Joe had his law degree, would he and Neilia make their home in New York, or in Delaware? Joe's family, of course, hoped the young couple would settle near them. Joseph Biden urged his son to apply to law firms in Wilmington.

Using his business connections, Joe's father got him a meeting with a friend of a friend, a superior court judge. The judge was impressed with Joe—"a sparkler," he called him later. On the spot, he arranged a job interview for Joe with the highly respected law firm of Prickett, Ward, Burt & Sanders.

At the lunch interview, Rod Ward kidded Joe about his so-so grades in law school. "Obviously, you're hoping to get a job based on your good looks." Joe assumed that meant he didn't have a chance of being hired.

But actually, Ward was impressed with this young man's intelligence and likability. Also, Joe had excellent letters of recommendation from his law school professors. "Mr. Biden has shown himself to possess the confidence and capabilities which would enable him to become an outstanding trial attorney," Dean Robert Miller had written. So the law firm offered Joe Biden a job, although at a low starting salary.

In the summer of 1968, the young Bidens threw a big farewell barbecue for their friends and neighbors in Syracuse. Then they moved to Wilmington, where they rented a small farmhouse in Mayfield, where Joe's parents still lived. Joe and Neilia started looking for a house to buy. Neilia was pregnant with their first child, and it seemed that they were well launched on their plan for their life together.

Joe took up his job at Prickett, Ward, Burt & Sanders, but he stayed with them for only six months. He worked hard for the law firm, but he felt more and more uncomfortable with their politics. He was a Democrat, sympathizing with labor unions and civil rights. The members of the firm, in contrast, were Republicans, and their main clients were wealthy corporations. Joe didn't tell his bosses that he would never vote for Richard Nixon, the Republican candidate for president in 1968.

Joe finally decided to quit the day he watched William Prickett, one of the partners, argue a case at the courthouse in downtown Wilmington. Prickett was defending the Catalytic Construction Company against a welder who had been badly burned on the job. The lawyer's argument to the judge was that the injuries were partly the welder's own fault. It was a perfectly legal defense, and Joe knew that Prickett was just doing his job. The judge would probably dismiss the suit.

But Joe left the courthouse sickened from watching the welder's family, especially the wife. She was about the same age as Neilia, and she'd looked so crushed by the unfairness of the law. Her husband was crippled and disfigured for life—but they would get nothing.

William Prickett invited Joe out to lunch that day, but the young lawyer made up an excuse. Instead he walked across Rodney Square to the state of Delaware's Office of the Public Defender. There he signed up to work as a lawyer for clients like the welder, who could not afford to pay legal fees.

In his new job, most of Joe's clients were African

Americans from the inner city. Many of them were surprised that this young "honky," their insulting name for a white man, sincerely wanted to offer them their legal right to defense in court.

Working as a public defender part-time, Joe Biden also started his own law firm in 1969. He talked Dave Walsh, his best friend from Archmere Academy, into going into business as his partner. He also persuaded Jack Owens, his best friend from law school, to move to Wilmington and join his firm.

Joe gave his best for his clients, but he was still determined to go into politics. He and Neilia had many passionate discussions about their future, and Neilia wished that Joe would keep practicing law. She imagined him becoming a judge—and someday, a Supreme Court justice. But Joe had a different vision for himself, and she accepted that.

Joe had been brought up on the importance of politics, first at Grandpop Finnegan's kitchen table and later at the Biden family's dinner-table discussions. And he could see, in his daily life in Wilmington, what a difference one person in a position of power could make. Because of Charles Layman Terry Jr., the governor of Delaware, soldiers patrolled the streets of Wilmington with drawn bayonets.

# 1968: Year of Turmoil

President Lyndon Johnson was elected by a landslide in 1964, and he had high hopes of transforming the country into a "Great Society." He did achieve some important goals, including the establishment of Medicare—health insurance for the elderly. However, Johnson's accomplishments were overshadowed as he led the US deep into the quagmire of the Vietnam War. By 1968, thousands of young American men had fled to Canada to avoid the military draft, or just refused to serve. Thousands more people marched in front of the White House and across the country to protest what they saw as a senseless, brutal, costly war. So many Democrats turned against the president and the war that on March 31, Johnson announced that he would not run for reelection.

But that was not the end of the turmoil. Only a few days later, on April 4, the civil rights leader Martin Luther King Jr. was assassinated in Memphis, Tennessee. Riots broke out in cities across the country, including Washington, DC, Chicago, and even Wilmington, Delaware.

Meanwhile, presidential candidates were

running for their parties' nominations. One of the Democratic front-runners was Senator Robert F. Kennedy, brother of the assassinated president John F. Kennedy. On June 5, just after winning the California primary election, Robert Kennedy also was shot by an assassin.

In August the Democratic National Convention met in Chicago and nominated Hubert Humphrey, Lyndon Johnson's vice president, as their candidate. Outside the convention, angry protesters of the Vietnam War confronted police and National Guard troops, and an ugly brawl took place on national television. The Republicans had already nominated Richard M. Nixon, who promised to win the war in Vietnam and restore law and order in the US. That November, Nixon narrowly won the election from Humphrey as well as from a third-party candidate, former governor George C. Wallace of Alabama.

After the assassination of Dr. Martin Luther King Jr. in the spring of 1968, riots had broken out in Wilmington's inner city, where the majority of residents were African American. Governor Terry's

solution to the unrest was to send in the National
Guard.

The riots subsided, and the mayor of Wilmington
asked the governor to call off the guard. But Governor
Terry kept the military occupation in the Black
district of Wilmington for the next nine months. Joe
Biden's sympathies were with the residents of the
Black neighborhoods, whose streets were shadowed
by white soldiers with rifles. The residents lived under
curfews and with the fear that their children would be
accidentally shot. They were people like the lifeguards
Joe had worked with the summer after his freshman
year in college.

While Joe's law career was taking off, the young
Biden family was growing, just as Joe and Neilia
had planned. Their first baby, Joseph Robinette
Biden III, called Beau, was born on February 3,
1969. Only a year and a day later, Beau's brother,
Robert Hunter Biden, was born on February 4,
1970. More than ever, Joe and Neilia were eager to
find the right house.

Joe had been fascinated with houses ever since
he was a boy. As a student at Archmere, riding the
school bus, he'd noticed the difference between his

own neighborhood and the neighborhoods of many of his classmates. The roads in Mayfield were as straight as tic-tac-toe lines, and the small, cheaply built houses perched on flat, bare lots. In the more attractive neighborhoods, majestic oaks and elms lined the curving roads, shading solid, spacious homes.

Now Biden felt close to realizing his dream home, and he and Neilia spent weekends driving around the outskirts of Wilmington, looking at real estate. With a loan from Neilia's father, they bought a small house in nearby Newark, Delaware—not to live in, but to fix up, rent, and eventually sell for a profit. Joe and Neilia found a house they liked for themselves in the Brandywine Springs Manor section of Wilmington. But they decided Joe's parents should buy it instead, while Joe and Neilia bought the Bidens' house in Mayfield.

Instead of living in the Mayfield house, Joe and Neilia rented it out also. Then they bought a farm that had possibilities of becoming their ideal home. There was a house they could enlarge for their growing family and visitors, and a big piece of land with room for other family members to build their homes. In the meantime, they rented the farm, as well, to college students. Now they were paying three mortgages.

To save money, Joe, Neilia, and the babies moved into a cottage on the grounds of the Country Club Swimming Pool. They could live there for free if Joe managed the swimming pool. For a person with Joe's energy and ambition, it was no problem to squeeze pool management into his crowded schedule. "I was probably the only working attorney in Delaware who lifeguarded on Saturdays," he joked later.

The Bidens were doing quite a real-estate juggling act. And it would get even more complicated with Joe's first dive into politics.

Joe's opening came when John Daniello, a Democrat on the New Castle County Council, decided to run for Congress in 1970. The problem was, Daniello didn't want to leave his seat on the county council unguarded, for a Republican to win. Daniello had heard that Joe Biden was smart, popular, and ambitious. So he and others in the Democratic Forum, a group working to get the Delaware Democratic Party concerned about civil rights, asked Joe to run for county council in 1970.

For several reasons, Biden wasn't eager to run. He wasn't very interested in county affairs, like local construction regulations. Besides, New Castle County was heavily Republican, so his chances of getting elected weren't good. And anyway, he yearned to jump straight into national politics, where he could have a say on big issues like the ongoing Vietnam War.

But as Daniello pointed out, Biden had to start somewhere, just to get his name known to voters. So Joe checked the idea out with Neilia, who had a good instinctive understanding of politics. She said, "Let's try it."

And Joe's sister, Valerie, enthusiastically agreed to manage his campaign. If anything, she was a fiercer competitor than Joe. As Joe noted later in his first memoir, "Valerie Biden did not go into any race to lose."

Valerie was only twenty-six, but she was already an experienced campaign manager. She'd run Joe's campaigns since he'd been elected president of the junior class at Archmere, and he'd always won. Now Val set up a campaign center in their parents' basement. From the public voting records, she gathered a database that included every registered voter in the district so that she knew which people were likely to vote Democratic. She organized a small army of volunteers, including her two younger brothers, to help voters get to the polls.

Meanwhile, Joe went door to door in the Democratic neighborhoods, introducing himself to the voters. But he also knocked on doors in the Republican precincts, confident that he could win voters over one by one. With his savvy about real estate, Joe knew what middle-class Republican voters cared about. They wanted to keep developers from building on all the open spaces, to keep the county budget tight, and to support the police.

On Election Day in November 1970, almost every single Democratic candidate in the state of Delaware, including John Daniello for Congress, lost their race. But Joe Biden won his county council seat by two thousand votes.

At the same time that Joe Biden was jump-starting his political career, he was also building the family life he wanted. Interviewed after the election by a reporter for the *Wilmington Evening Journal*, he said, "The most important thing to me without question is to be a good father."

Soon after Biden took his seat on the New Castle County Council, Neilia was pregnant for the third time. The Bidens definitely needed a bigger house than the pool cottage, where little Beau was sleeping in a closet. After long searching, Joe and Neilia found their ideal house in North Star, a village only a few miles from the border between Delaware and Pennsylvania. This house, built in 1723, stood on four acres of land. Through complicated financial arrangements, they managed to sell their three rental properties and buy their dream house in the spring of 1971.

Unfortunately, this perfect Colonial house was not in the county council district that Joe Biden represented. He couldn't move there and still keep his seat on the council. But Joe's parents had just moved into a house that *was* in Joe's district. So all he had to do was talk his dumbfounded mother and father into moving again—to North Star. "You'd really like it," he urged. "It'd just be for a year or so."

Three days later, Joe's brother Jimmy moved Joseph and Jean Biden's belongings into the house in North Star. Joe, Neilia, Beau, and Hunter would live in the senior Bidens' house for the next year, until after the 1972 election. On November 8, 1971, Joe and Neilia's baby girl was born, and they named her Naomi Christina.

Joe Biden could have been satisfied with this good start to his political career. But he was already looking ahead, thinking of running for the Senate in 1972. Not the Delaware *state* senate, a reasonable goal for an ambitious young man, but the United States Senate.

This would be a huge leap, from county councilman to US senator. To make the leap even harder, the senator up for reelection in 1972 was the popular Republican James Caleb Boggs. Boggs had had a long, successful political career, and every voter in Delaware knew who he was. Why would they vote for an unknown young Democrat instead? Biden wouldn't even turn thirty, the minimum age for a US senator, until thirteen days after the election.

But Joe Biden was thinking about his next step in politics as carefully as he used to figure out plays on the football field, or as he planned his rhythm and word choice to avoid stuttering. For one thing, he was unlikely to get reelected to the county council. The precincts were being redistricted by the Republicans so as to favor Republican candidates even more. Joe had actually heard them laughing about this legal but unfair trick.

Joe understood that the gap between county councilman and US senator might be too wide to bridge. He would have preferred to run for the US House of Representatives, a smaller gap. But the current representative in his district was Pierre S. du Pont IV.

DuPont Chemical was a major industry in Delaware, wealthy and influential. Joe didn't think he'd stand a chance against Congressman du Pont, backed by the money and prestige of his family's company.

Although Joe was aiming for bigger things than the New Castle County Council, he did apply his talents and energy for the county during his two years in office. He fought, as he'd promised, against development that would break up the communities of Wilmington and build over open space. He prevented the corporate giant Shell Oil from polluting the environment with refineries on the Delaware seashore.

All this work was for causes that Biden sincerely believed in. It also made him known as a politician who was out to serve the people. And at every public appearance, Joe, naturally outgoing and likable, generated good publicity for himself. So did his young, appealing family.

The Democratic Party in Delaware had been weak and disorganized for years, but now there was a movement afoot to reform and strengthen it. Joe Biden, a young, talented, ambitious politician, had a lot to offer the Democrats. Henry Topel, the chair of the state Democratic Party, was impressed with Joe's youth following. They couldn't vote yet, but they'd already played an important part in Joe's campaign for county councilman.

In fact, Topel's own son David was one of the teenagers in Valerie Biden's political network. David contacted high schools all over Delaware, arranging for Joe to speak to the students in classrooms and assemblies. Joe spoke passionately about how the US should end the Vietnam War, and the students responded eagerly. They wanted to do something— they only needed to be asked. Senator Boggs supported President Nixon's running of the war, so these young people were inspired to help the Democrats beat Boggs.

Henry Topel could see that Joe Biden and his army of young activists could be a big help to the Democrats. He put Biden on the state party reform commission. This job gave Biden the chance to travel around Delaware and meet important Democrats outside the county of New Castle.

As the commission searched for the right person to run for the Senate in 1972, Biden didn't push the idea of himself as the candidate. But by the summer of 1971, the Delaware Democratic Party had run out of other likely candidates. They'd asked the former governor, the chief justice of the Delaware Supreme

Court, and several others, but none of them wanted to run against Caleb Boggs.

Finally, during a convention of the state party, Joe Biden heard a knock on the door of his motel room. He was in the middle of shaving, wearing shorts, but he let in Henry Topel and Bert Carvel, former governor of Delaware. They'd come to a decision: they wanted *him* to run against Boggs for the Senate. The Democrats needed to run a candidate, no matter how hopeless the chances looked. And nobody else wanted to be the "sacrificial lamb," doomed to lose.

Joe said that he needed time to think it over. But he'd already been planning for this.

# Chapter 6

# Triumph and Tragedy

For the second time, Joe Biden's whole family plunged into a political struggle. This time, the stakes were much higher. If Joe was elected to the US Senate, he'd have the chance to influence the big issues he cared about so much: The Vietnam War. Women's rights. Civil rights. The environment. The problem of crime.

Neilia was all in. She'd let go her dream of Joe becoming a Supreme Court justice. Now she advised him to give up his law practice, although it was their main source of income. Even with Joe's unusual energy, she pointed out, he couldn't run his law firm, do his work as county councilman, *and* run for a national office.

As for Valerie Biden, of course she'd be Joe's manager for this campaign too. Her husband, Bruce

Saunders, oversaw the campaign budget. Joe's brother Jimmy accepted the job of raising money — they estimated that running for the Senate would cost Joe $150,000. Frankie, still a teenager, could help gather the high school volunteers.

The campaign gathered momentum. Joe Biden's energy and joy were contagious, especially for the young volunteers. They felt like part of the family. And the Bidens treated them that way, encouraging the young people to drop by to play touch football and swim in the pool.

Jean Biden worried that running for the Senate would ruin her son's so-far brilliant career. But Joe assured her that even if he lost the race, he'd win. The campaign would get him known throughout the state of Delaware, and maybe even get him some national publicity. As his mother had to agree, people who got to know Joe Biden almost always liked him.

Besides, Joe intended to win. He was confident that he could charm voters into giving him a chance.

Before Biden even announced that he was running for the US Senate, his campaign launched a series of "coffees" — meetings in private homes — around the state of Delaware. At that time, not many women worked outside the home, so they were able to attend daytime meetings. Each coffee was Joe's chance to introduce himself to thirty people at a time, in person, and to explain why he was running for senator. And—very important—these meetings were a chance to listen to Delaware residents' concerns.

During the fall of 1971, Joe's campaign organized hundreds of neighborhood coffees. They found a hostess in each neighborhood, invited likely guests, and provided coffee and doughnuts. Twice a week, Joe attended ten coffees a day, beginning at eight o'clock.

As Joe arrived at the first meeting, Val would go on to set up the nine o'clock coffee, while Neilia would set up the ten o'clock. Jean Biden would wrap up at the end of the eight o'clock coffee and then leave to set up the eleven o'clock. And so on, the candidate and his team leapfrogging through the day.

Beau, Hunter, and baby Naomi were on the campaign trail too, although they were too little to know it. "We just carried them from house to house like footballs in wicker baskets," Biden wrote later.

Delaware is such a small state that you can drive its length in only two hours. So thousands of voters had the chance to see Joe's winning smile and hear his persuasive words, close and personal. They felt his warmth, and his concern for their concerns. Reporters began to take notice of Joe Biden, calling him a "joyous campaigner" and a "rising star" in the Democratic Party.

It was easy for Joe Biden to be likable, but he also intended to know what he was talking to voters about. He wanted to be the best-informed candidate. So Neilia put on Sunday night spaghetti dinners at their house, inviting scholars from the University of Pennsylvania and the University of Delaware. These dinners were like seminars, where Joe and his team could learn from the experts about important issues: the ongoing Vietnam War, problems of drug abuse, the environment, and crime.

Meanwhile, Jimmy Biden, only twenty-three at the time, traveled around asking for money. In Delaware, he didn't stand a chance of getting funds from the state Democratic Party. They were sure that Biden was going to lose, and they were pouring their money into the governor's race.

But outside of Delaware, Jimmy got more interest. He flew around the country, as far as Alaska and California, to find donors. He saw his job as a salesman with the best possible product—his brother Joe. "In sales," he explained later, "you have to believe in your product, and I was a believer. How were they going to say no?"

And Joe, with his loyal, hardworking family and friends, had the best possible volunteer team. But at a certain point, the Bidens realized that they needed a professional campaign consultant. Joe thought he'd found the ideal consultant in Jack Owens, his best friend from law school. Jack had already worked on two successful political races in Pennsylvania.

So Jack joined the "Biden for Senator" campaign — but only two months later, he had to quit. Campaign manager Valerie couldn't stand Jack now any better than she had on that blind date several years before in Syracuse. The bad feeling was mutual. Jack dropped out, and Joe hired instead a young consultant from Boston, John Marttila.

Another professional who joined the campaign was Patrick Caddell, a young pollster. His first poll for Biden, early in 1972, showed Joe losing to Boggs by a landslide. Joe exclaimed, "Oh my God, I'm going to get killed!" But Neilia got him to calm down and pay attention to the details of Caddell's explanation. The pollster said there were hopeful signs—the numbers could change as the campaign went on.

On March 20, 1972, at the Hotel Du Pont in downtown Wilmington, Joseph R. Biden Jr. officially announced his candidacy for the US Senate. Although Biden spoke respectfully of his opponent, Senator Boggs, he suggested that the sixty-two-year-old politician was out of tune with the times. Americans were sick of the war in Vietnam, and people in Delaware in particular had lost many young soldiers to the war. Boggs, a Republican, would not criticize President Nixon for continuing the war. But Biden said bluntly that it was "a horrendous waste of time, money, and lives."

During the campaign Biden was frank with his audiences about where he stood on the issues, and he didn't necessarily agree with every liberal position. He did not favor legalizing marijuana. Although he was for racial integration, he thought school busing to achieve integration was a mistake.

If he was honest with voters, Joe believed, they would trust him. And trust was especially important to Americans disillusioned over the Vietnam War. Many felt that the government, whether Democratic or Republican, had been lying to them for years.

Since Joe Biden was hardly known outside of Wilmington, he hoped to persuade some national Democratic politicians to endorse him — to announce publicly that they supported his campaign. That would get Delaware voters to take him more seriously. With this purpose, Biden traveled to Washington, DC, to visit Mike Mansfield, majority leader of the US Senate.

Mansfield wasn't willing to actually endorse Joe Biden, since Caleb Boggs was a longtime colleague of Mansfield's in the Senate. But Mansfield agreed to have his picture taken with Biden in the grand reception room of the Senate, and to say something nice that Biden's campaign could quote in their flyers. A few other Democratic bigwigs, including Senator Ted Kennedy of Massachusetts, also joined the photo op in the Senate reception room.

As Joe Biden went from neighborhood coffees to polka dances in the Polish sections to high school football games, Senator Caleb Boggs hardly campaigned at all. Why should he? By September, the polls still showed him winning easily over the upstart Biden. Senator Boggs turned down a chance to debate with Biden on TV. Boggs had spent only $3,000 to this point, compared with Biden's $50,000, although Boggs's campaign had plenty of money.

Overall, 1972 looked to be a good year for Republicans. It was also a presidential election year.

The prediction was that President Richard Nixon would easily win reelection over his Democratic rival, Senator George McGovern of South Dakota.

The Biden campaign desperately needed money, especially for radio advertisements during the final weeks. But there were lines Joe refused to cross. One time, he and Jimmy went to a meeting with a group of Delaware's wealthiest businessmen. The brothers hoped that these men would donate $20,000 to pay for the radio ads.

The multimillionaires were friendly, but Joe Biden's hackles went up when they asked him what he thought about tax reform. President Nixon had proposed a tax reform that would increase their profits, and Biden had come out against it. Now he sensed that these men wanted him to take back what he'd said on the campaign trail. Instead Joe repeated what he'd said before about tax reform.

Jimmy was disgusted. He thought Joe had lost the election with his stubbornness, and he didn't speak to his brother on the drive home. But Joe took out a second mortgage on his house for $20,000 to pay for the radio spots.

Whether a donor represented big business or labor unions, Biden felt exactly the same about anyone who wanted to tell him how to vote. One time, Jimmy managed to get a promise from the president of the machinists' union to donate $5,000. But when Joe and Jimmy went to Washington, DC, to pick up the check, Joe almost blew it.

The union president pressured Joe to say that if it came to a vote in the Senate, he'd vote in favor of the union. To Jimmy's horror, Joe rudely told him what he could do with his check, and he walked out of the office. Jimmy himself quietly accepted the check.

In the last five or six weeks of the campaign, Patrick Caddell's polls showed Joe Biden's numbers rising. Biden's team worked feverishly to promote their candidate. Joe's consultant Marttila wrote and produced tabloid "newspapers" describing Biden in glowing terms. Marttila had the papers run off in Boston, Massachusetts, and trucked down to Wilmington overnight each Friday.

Early Saturday morning, bundles were dropped off at garages in neighborhoods all over Delaware. Valerie's corps of young volunteers delivered the papers to 350,000 homes. They were rewarded with orange juice, doughnuts—and pride at being part of this exciting movement.

Joe himself kept on walking around neighborhoods, knocking on doors, asking voters to choose him on Election Day. Neilia walked with him, whispering into his ear important details about the people approaching him on the sidewalk, so he could make that personal connection. Joe kept on speaking to any group that would listen.

The polls still predicted Senator Boggs winning over Biden, but the gap was growing narrower. The Republicans began to worry. In the *Wilmington News Journal*, a headline read, 'SACRIFICIAL LAMB' MAY REWRITE SCRIPT. Ten days before the election, the polls showed the two candidates running neck and neck.

Tuesday, November 7, was Election Day. That night Joe Biden, with his extended family and campaign team, waited in the ballroom of the Hotel Du Pont for the results. At last the votes from a working-class Polish neighborhood put Joe over the top. Senator Boggs called to concede the election.

Joe was stunned. The whole room was silent for a moment, as if no one could believe they'd really won. Then Neilia's father, Robert Hunter, broke the silence with a joke. "Well, Joe, if my daughter has to be married to a Democrat, he might as well be a United States senator."

And Joe really *was* senator-elect Biden! That night, he and Neilia were too keyed up to sleep. They lay in bed talking about their future. Everything was still working out the way they'd planned before they were married: their children, their house, Joe's career in politics. Soon they'd move on to the next step, their exciting new life together in Washington, DC.

On November 20, 1972, Joe Biden turned thirty—and finally he was old enough to become a US senator. The Bidens celebrated Joe's birthday, along with his victory in the Senate race, with a big party at the Pianni Grill in Wilmington. It was a newsworthy event, with a TV crew to film Joe and Neilia cutting his birthday cake together.

In the following weeks, Joe felt like he was sailing along, confident and clearheaded. Now that he'd won, even more people were donating to his campaign, so he could pay back the second mortgage on the North Star house. He and Neilia were swept up in plans and arrangements. In two short months, they needed to buy a house in Washington, the right house near the right future school for Beau, Hunter, and Naomi.

Senator Biden would need people to run his office, so he had job seekers to interview. Fortunately, he already had an experienced chief of staff, Wes Barthelmes. He also wanted to get a head start on good relations with his fellow senators, so he began calling on other senators to introduce himself.

Joe Biden would be the youngest member of the new Senate, and the sixth-youngest ever to serve in the Senate. And he looked even younger than he was. Joe joked that his colleagues would think he was a page, one of the boys who delivered mail around the Senate.

Senators' offices were assigned according to rank, and Joe's rank was right at the bottom. So he was assigned a little office on the sixth floor of the Dirksen Senate Office Building, the farthest away from the Capitol. Senator Robert Byrd of West Virginia let Biden use some office space until he could move into his own humble quarters.

Neilia often came along to Washington with Joe to house-hunt. They planned to keep the North Star house, but they wanted to live right in Washington, where Joe would be working. They were still short on cash, but Neilia's father offered to lend them the down payment. They found a house they liked, near a school they liked, and they made an offer.

That weekend Joe and Neilia finally took time to savor this point in their lives. They agreed that their beautiful house in Wilmington, in North Star, would be their real family home. They'd spend every weekend there, and they'd celebrate all the holidays and special occasions there, surrounded by family and friends.

On Monday morning, December 18, Joe took the Amtrak train to Washington. Neilia had decided not to go with him this time. She had some major Christmas shopping to do, and Christmas was only a week away. She packed the three children into the station wagon and went off to look for a Christmas tree. The following day, Neilia planned, she'd go to Washington with Joe and sign the papers on the house they were buying.

That afternoon, Joe was sitting with Valerie in his borrowed office in Washington when the phone rang. Valerie picked it up. It was Jimmy, calling from Wilmington. As Valerie listened, her face turned white.

Valerie hung up and tried to break the news to Joe gently. "There's been a slight accident. Nothing to be worried about. But we ought to go home."

Somehow Joe knew—from Val's expression, or her tone of voice—what the news really was. "She's dead, isn't she?"

They flew back to Wilmington and rushed to the

hospital, where Joe learned the full story. After Neilia had driven off on her Christmas errands, her station wagon had collided with a tractor-trailer. Her car rolled into a ditch. She and Naomi, the baby, were killed. Beau's leg and some other bones were broken, and Hunter had a cracked skull.

"I could not speak," Joe wrote years later, "only felt this hollow core grow in my chest, like I was going to be sucked inside a black hole."

The next several days he spent at the hospital, never leaving the boys. He was in a weird state, dozing off now and then and waking to a nightmare reality. Neilia, the love of his life, the partner of his dreams, was gone. The happy family they'd grown together was shattered: the baby dead, Beau in a full body cast, Hunter with a fractured skull and possibly brain-damaged. There was a part of Joe that wanted to die too—but then remembered that Beau and Hunter needed him more than ever.

What pulled Joe through the ordeal, he remembered later, was his family. Someone—Valerie, Jimmy, their mother—was always there to support him. As Joe's vigil at the hospital dragged on, he began going out for nighttime walks around the city, trying to walk off his growing rage.

Jimmy went along to keep an eye on him, fearing that his brother was looking for a fight. And Joe would have been glad for an excuse to punch someone, as he admitted later. He was shocked at how angry he was, even angry at God. "I felt God had played a horrible trick on me."

Now Joe Biden's seat in the Senate, and all his plans for the great things he'd expected to achieve there, meant nothing to him. The only future he could imagine was one of taking care of his sons. He called Mike Mansfield, the majority leader of the Senate, and told him he was giving up his Senate seat. Biden had already told the governor of Delaware, who would appoint someone to fill in temporarily.

# Chapter 7

# Young Senator Biden

In Joe Biden's black mood after the accident, nothing mattered except four-year-old Beau and three-year-old Hunter. He didn't want to go on living, but he would live for them. At least the boys were recovering well. The doctors assured Joe that Beau's broken bones would heal, and Hunter's brain had not been damaged.

At first Joe assumed that the best thing for his sons would be for him to stay home with them. But when he talked to his friends and family about the future, his mind began to change. There was his father's advice from long ago, which had always served Joe well: "If you get knocked down, get up."

Valerie, Joe's first best friend and trusted advisor, argued that he didn't have to choose between the Senate and his sons. She and her husband, Bruce, would move into the North Star house with Joe. She would quit her teaching job at Wilmington Friends School and take care of the boys full-time.

And Joe didn't need to move to Washington, DC, as he and Neilia had planned. Washington was only a train ride away from Wilmington. Senator Biden could live at home and commute to work, while taking his boys to school every morning and tucking them into bed every night.

Val loved her nephews and wanted the best for them. But she also believed it would be best for her brother to plunge into the demanding work of the Senate. It would give him some sense of purpose, a way to recover from his crushing tragedy. And it would be good for Beau and Hunter to see their father following through on his commitment to the people of Delaware.

Meanwhile, Senate Majority Leader Mike Mansfield would not give up on Joe, and he continued to call him every day. He was sympathetic with Biden's loss, but he was determined to keep him in the Senate. He talked about the votes he was counting on Biden to support. He tempted Biden with the promise of a place on the Senate Democratic Steering Committee—an unusual favor for a freshman senator.

Finally, the wily Mansfield told Joe that by taking his seat in the Senate, he would be honoring Neilia's memory. That was the clinching argument for Joe. Neilia had worked for this victory as hard as he had. She had believed in him and encouraged him, from that first day on the beach in Nassau. For Neilia's sake, he could at least try.

By the beginning of 1973, Joe Biden had agreed to serve in the Senate for at least six months. But he refused to travel to Washington to be sworn into office in the Senate Chamber, as was customary. Hunter was back home, but Beau was still in the hospital, and Joe wouldn't leave him. So Mike Mansfield sent the secretary of the Senate to the Wilmington General Hospital to administer the oath to Joe.

On January 5 a crowd of witnesses and TV crews watched the ceremony in the chapel of the hospital. Joseph and Jean Biden were there, as well as Neilia's parents from upstate New York. Beau, his leg in a cast, was wheeled into the room. Hunter perched on his brother's bed.

After taking his oath, Joe made a promise to his audience: If, after six months in the Senate, he felt that he couldn't be a good father as well as a good senator, he would resign.

In the following weeks and months, Joe took up his new routine. Early every morning he'd get Beau and Hunter up. Driving the boys to school, Joe encouraged them to sing along with the radio.

Their favorite song, by Elton John, was "Crocodile Rock." The three of them rode along, shouting at the top of their lungs, "'But the biggest kick I ever got / Was doing a thing called the Crocodile Rock.'" After dropping Beau and Hunter off at school, Joe rode the Amtrak train from Wilmington to Washington.

He had explained to Beau and Hunter that they were allowed to call him at work anytime. And he instructed his staff in Washington to interrupt him if one of the boys called. He'd always take the call, no matter what vital Senate business he was in the middle of.

Joe also let Beau and Hunter come to work with him whenever they wanted, so some days the three of them rode the train to Washington. They could stay in his office playing quietly, or go to the Senate gym, or listen to hearings. Sometimes, during a staff meeting, one of the boys would sit on his lap. They knew not to bother their father, and Joe's office staff helped to look after the boys.

At the end of the Senate's workday, other senators often went out for dinner together, or to one of the many parties and receptions in Washington. But Senator Biden hurried down Capitol Hill to Union Station and caught the train back to Wilmington. Usually he'd arrive home in time to put the boys to bed. Even when he arrived after bedtime, he'd always go kiss them good night.

Beau remembered, years afterward, how his father used to jump into bed with him and Hunter, hugging and kissing them. The young boys knew that Dad had an important job. But they also knew that *they* were more important to him than anything else in the world.

And Beau and Hunter were unusually close, even for brothers. Hunter would say later that his first memory was of waking up in a hospital bed after the tragic accident. Beau, in the bed next to him, turned to his younger brother and said, "I love you, I love you, I love you."

## The US Senate

In the Senate, one of the two houses of Congress, each state is represented by two senators. This is different from the House of Representatives, where states are represented according to population. For instance, the tiny state of Delaware sends only one delegate to the House, while the large state of Texas sends thirty-six.

Besides working with the House of Representatives to develop and pass laws, the Senate has the power to "advise and consent" when the president appoints members of the Cabinet or justices to the Supreme Court. The president must also get the Senate's approval for treaties with foreign countries.

The Democratic and the Republican Parties each elect their leaders in the Senate. The leader of the party in the majority has considerable power, including the power to bring bills up for debate—or not bring them up, which can kill a bill without even a vote. The majority leader also has the important right to speak first, before any other senator, to offer amendments, or motions to reconsider.

But the minority party has the right to *filibuster* a bill, to keep debate going in order to delay a vote. If they can keep talking long enough, they can sometimes prevent a bill from ever coming up for a vote. However, the majority can stop a filibuster through *cloture*. Cloture requires that a supermajority—or sixty out of the one hundred senators—vote to end the debate.

At the Capitol, several senators besides Mike Mansfield did their best to draw Joe Biden into the life of the Senate. Hubert Humphrey of Minnesota, formerly President Lyndon Johnson's vice president, had already called Joe many times while Beau and Hunter were in the hospital. Now Humphrey made a point of greeting Joe enthusiastically on the Senate floor. He often stopped by Joe's office, although it was out of his way, to ask how he and his boys were doing.

Senator Ted Kennedy of Massachusetts, younger brother of former president John F. Kennedy, also dropped into Biden's out-of-the-way office. He took Joe to the Senate gym and introduced him to famous senators in the steam baths.

In those days, the US Senate was in some ways like a men's club. There were no women senators, since Republican Margaret Chase Smith of Maine had lost reelection in 1972, and only one African American,

Republican Edward Brooke of Massachusetts. Among themselves, senators were generally friendly and civil, even with political enemies. Two senators with opposite political views might debate each other bitterly on the Senate floor but leave the chamber slapping each other on the back and joking.

From the beginning of his political career, Joe Biden had been open about his support for civil rights. Some of the Southern Democratic senators, on the other hand, were known as "Dixiecrats" for their defense of racial segregation. One of them was John Stennis of Mississippi.

Stennis had fought steadily against the civil rights movement during his long career in the Senate. However, he was perfectly courteous to the new senator from Delaware. He even made a point of congratulating Biden on his first speech in the Senate Chamber.

Senator James Eastland, also of Mississippi, was openly racist. He firmly believed that the white race was superior to the Black race, and that the races should be kept apart. However, Joe Biden thought he had something to learn from the older senator. After all, Eastland had served in Congress since 1929. And Joe had a talent for finding the issues that he agreed on with his political opponents, in order to work with them.

Besides, Joe liked Senator Eastland's dry sense of humor. According to Eastland, the most significant change in the Senate, in his long career, was air-conditioning. He explained that in the old days, the Senate Chamber had skylights in the ceiling. So in the spring, the chamber would heat up like a greenhouse, and the Senate would adjourn for the summer. "Then we put in air conditionin', stayed year round, and ruined America."

In spite of friendly outreach from his colleagues, Joe had to force himself to plod through the days. He was determined to do his job in the Senate, but he took no joy in it. He existed in a dull, numb state, broken by stabs of unbearable pain. His purpose each day was only to get through it and go back home to Beau and Hunter.

Joe Biden's first appearance on the floor of the Senate Chamber should have been a moment of high triumph. That morning, one of the Capitol policemen stepped forward, grinning, to congratulate him. "Senator Biden, do you remember me?" It was the same officer who, almost ten years before, had seized an unescorted college student named Joe and hauled him down to the basement for questioning. Now he told Biden, "I'm happy you're back."

Sadly, at this point Joe Biden could not be happy about much of anything. His chief of staff, Wes Barthelmes, became concerned that Joe was eating lunch by himself in his office every day. Barthelmes had to explain that it was part of Biden's job to join his fellow senators for lunch. Lunch in the Senate wasn't just a meal; it was a chance to get to know the people he had to work with. He needed to establish those personal relationships, sooner rather than later.

Normally, Joe Biden was a natural social animal. He loved meeting new people, getting to know them, making friends. And he understood perfectly well what his chief of staff was saying. But these days, he didn't want to be around people who would either pity him or avoid him. He just wanted to stay in his office and spend his lunchtime calling home.

After a few weeks, Biden did allow Barthelmes to take him down to the dining room in the Dirksen building. There his chief of staff spotted Senator John McClellan of Arkansas, the chair of the powerful Appropriations Committee. Barthelmes pushed Biden to go over and introduce himself.

McClellan, like everyone else in the Senate, had heard about Joe's tragic loss. But he didn't either pity Joe or try to avoid him. "Oh, you're the guy from Delaware? Lost your wife and kid, huh?"

Joe stood dumbstruck by the harsh words. The older senator added, "Only one thing to do. Bury yourself in work."

As Joe found out, McClellan knew what he was talking about. Early in his political career, his wife had died of spinal meningitis. Several years later, a son had died of the same disease. And later, two more of his sons had died.

Joe Biden would never get to be close friends with the much older McClellan, but his blunt talk gave Joe a little perspective on his grief. And he learned that there were other senators struggling with personal tragedy. The wife of Senator Birch Bayh of Indiana was suffering from breast cancer, which would kill her several years later. Senator Stuart Symington of Missouri had lost his wife the year before.

Meanwhile, Majority Leader Mike Mansfield was still looking out for Joe Biden. He asked the young senator to come by his office once a week, to report on how he was settling into the Senate. Although

Mansfield, as leader, was responsible for bringing freshman senators along, Biden knew he was getting special treatment. "He was taking my pulse," Biden later said wryly, as if he were a patient in a hospital.

Senator Hubert Humphrey, also looking out for Biden, knew that Joe was especially interested in foreign relations. Joe had hoped to be given a place on the prestigious Senate Foreign Relations Committee, but he was too new to the Senate for that.

However, there were other opportunities to travel abroad. Humphrey made sure that Biden was included in a delegation to a conference in Oxford, England. To top it off, Humphrey arranged for Joe's brother Jimmy to fly over to join him, and then take Joe on a five-day European vacation.

Jimmy joked that he was a "Senate wife" for Joe. He often rode the commuter train to Washington with his brother, to keep him company for the day. On weekends, Joe's friend Jack Owens would spend evenings with him, staying up late and talking. In Wilmington and in Washington, there was a strong network supporting Joe.

The first six months were up, and Joe Biden stayed in the Senate. He took on more responsibility for his party, especially campaigning for other candidates. Senators have six-year terms, but members of the House of Representatives have to run for reelection every two years.

So there were always a number of campaigns going on. There were always many candidates who needed help getting votes and raising money. The Democratic Congressional Campaign Committee sent Biden out on long speaking tours, covering the United States from Vermont to Hawaii.

In a way, it was a relief for Joe to travel. He hated to leave Beau and Hunter for these trips, but he could see that they were becoming more relaxed, more confident that he would always come back to them. And he was leaving them with a close and loving family. The boys' aunt Valerie took care of them. Their uncle Frank was always around, and their Biden grandparents not far away.

As for himself, Joe Biden slept better when he was on the road. The North Star house, his and Neilia's dream house, was now the house of lost dreams. He actually looked forward to trips so that he could get some rest. Also, it lifted his spirits to be helping other Democrats, speaking to audiences. He still had his gift of connecting with a crowd.

At home, as the boys settled into their new routine, Joe eased up a bit, too. In Washington, he made friends with a group of senators and their wives. After a time, he even accepted invitations to their monthly dinners.

In New Castle County, Delaware, the county council announced plans to build a new park of ten and a half acres. It would include a football field, a Little League baseball field, basketball courts, and bicycle racks. There would be a playground with equipment for younger children. The council, on which Joe Biden had started his political career, was naming the recreation area Neilia Hunter Biden Park.

At the beginning of Joe Biden's second year in Congress, the *San Francisco Chronicle* judged him to be one of the ten best-dressed men in the Senate. This honor was not huge, since the typical US senator was older, rumpled, and unfashionable. But it got Senator Biden some good publicity.

By this time, Biden had proven himself as a speaker who could raise funds for the Democrats. He still enjoyed making speeches, and his friendly personality came through to audiences. A rumor started that the Democratic Party might choose him as their candidate for president in the election of 1976.

That talk could easily have given the young, ambitious senator a swelled head, but he knew he wasn't yet qualified to run for president. "I don't have the experience or background," he told a TV interviewer in September 1974. Joe wanted to reassure the people of Delaware that he intended to represent his state in the Senate for years to come.

"If you hang around Washington," Biden explained, "it's easy to start thinking you're important, and so it is a blessing in disguise that I commute every day and get out of this city." He added, "I prefer being home with my kids, and that way I'm home with my constituents too."

Senate Majority Leader Mike Mansfield thought so well of Joe Biden that in 1975 he gave Biden a seat on the Foreign Relations Committee. Biden had been hoping for this assignment for two years, and he appreciated what a big favor it was for a junior senator like him. He was thrilled to attend his first meeting with the legendary secretary of state Henry Kissinger.

But Biden got off on the wrong foot that day. First he went to a room in the Dirksen Senate offices, only to discover that the Foreign Relations Committee meeting was in the Capitol instead. Late now, Biden rushed to the Capitol and the correct room—and was grabbed by an armed guard. "Where d'ya think you're goin', buddy?"

Waving his Senate ID at the guard, Biden plunged into the hearing room. In his hurry he slammed the door and bumped into the back of Kissinger's chair. Most people would have kept a low profile for the rest of the meeting, after such a bumbling entrance. But Biden soon raised his hand to ask a question.

Kissinger had assumed that this annoying young man was someone's assistant. "Mr. Chairman," he addressed acting chair Mansfield in his distinctive German-accented croak, "I thought no staff was allowed."

One of Kissinger's staff passed him an urgent note, informing him that the annoying young man was actually the junior senator from Delaware. "Oh," said Kissinger. "I apologize, Senator Bid-den."

Joe couldn't resist a teasing answer, pretending to mistake Kissinger for President Eisenhower's secretary of state in the 1950s: "No problem, Secretary Dulles."

# Chapter 8

# Jill

Joe Biden was building a reputation as "Amtrak Joe." Riding the train to Washington every day, he soon knew all the conductors, as well as the other regular passengers. Now and then he used the time, an hour and twenty minutes, to catch up on paperwork. But more often he spent the time talking.

Sometimes Beau and Hunter would ride with their father, and sometimes Joe Sr. would come along. He'd followed politics all his life, and he was deeply proud of his son the senator. He enjoyed sitting in on Joe's hearings and meetings.

Besides chatting, discussing, and arguing with his fellow passengers, Joe also liked to sketch designs for the perfect Biden home. Beau later remembered sitting on the train, watching his father draw plans for houses, as well as the grounds around them. Joe dreamed of a family house that would welcome the people he loved, all of them. It would be like his childhood home with his Finnegan grandparents in Scranton, only bigger and better.

In 1975, Valerie Biden was still in the North Star house with Joe, Beau, and Hunter, taking care of the boys. Her marriage to Bruce Saunders had broken up, and this year she got remarried—to Joe's good friend Jack Owens. The relationship that had started out ten years before, with that disastrous blind date in Syracuse, had completely turned around. Val had to admit that Neilia had been right to say, "If I could pick any guy in the world for you, it would be Jack Owens."

As Joe slowly recovered from the tragic loss of Neilia and their baby Naomi, he felt more and more that he no longer wanted to live in the North Star house. He started looking for a new house, and he found one he loved at first sight in the suburb of Greenville. It was a former Du Pont mansion with two separate wings—"one for me and one for Val," thought Biden. He knew that Valerie, even married to Jack, would still want to live in the same house with Beau and Hunter.

Joe Biden bought the Greenville house and began remodeling it. In later years, Beau had fond memories of weekend trips to the hardware store with his father. The family spent days planting trees, putting up a fence, painting rooms. Hunter remembered how his father would hold him out a high window so he could reach the eaves with a paintbrush.

Just as Joe had hoped, his new house welcomed a stream of family and friends. In fact, so many people were always coming and going that a friend named this Biden house "the Station."

Around Wilmington, Biden's neighbors and acquaintances thought of him as friendly, generous, helpful Joe. They knew that he was a senator, of course, but they also felt that he was one of them. His mother had brought him up to believe that he was the equal of anyone, but also that anyone was equal to him.

One day Biden happened to be driving through a neighborhood when he saw a boy snatch a woman's purse. As the boy started to run away, Joe jumped out of his car. He chased the boy through backyards and over fences, until the thief threw the purse down.

Joe returned the purse to the woman, who was overwhelmed by his gallantry. Thirty years later, she would still have that same purse. She expected Biden to become president someday, and she'd kept the rescued purse for him to sign when he was elected.

One Friday evening in March 1975, Joe happened to return from Washington to Wilmington by plane, instead of his usual train ride. As he walked through the airport, he noticed posters for the New Castle County parks. The posters showed different scenes around the park system, and the same beautiful, blond young woman appeared in several posters.

At home, Joe found his brothers waiting, with their dates, to go out with him. Frank suggested that Joe bring a date along too. He knew a young woman whom Joe was sure to like, he said, and he gave Joe her phone number.

Joe didn't feel like going on a date with someone new—he just wanted to spend time with his family that night. But the next day, after a good rest, he was curious about this young woman. Her name was Jill Jacobs. Frank had said, "She doesn't like politics," and for some reason that appealed to Joe. He gave her a call.

As it happened, Jill already had a date for Saturday night. But this roused Joe's competitive side, and he asked her to break her date. He was a US senator, he explained, and he only had this night in town. Joe's charm must have come through the phone, because Jill agreed to try to rearrange her schedule.

When Joe picked her up that night, he was startled to recognize the person who answered the door. It was the same beautiful woman he'd seen on the New Castle County Parks posters.

They drove to Philadelphia for dinner. Joe realized, as they talked, that Frank was right—Jill wasn't interested in politics. And she didn't seem impressed to be going out with a US senator.

She'd voted for him in 1972, though. That was the first time she'd ever voted, and she remembered going to senator-elect Biden's victory party at the Hotel Du Pont and shaking hands with him and his wife, Neilia. That fall, Jill had been a junior at the University of Delaware, Joe's old school. She was nine years younger than Joe.

Over dinner, Joe and Jill had much to talk about. She didn't ask him about his work in the Senate, or about famous people he'd met. They talked instead about their families, and people they both knew, and "about books and real life," as Biden wrote later.

Joe was immediately taken with Jill Jacobs.

This evening was the first time since Neilia's death that he'd been so happy in a woman's company. He asked her out the next night, and the one after that. Jill didn't point out that obviously he'd been fibbing about having only one night in town, but Joe could tell that she was amused.

Jill found a lot to like about Joe, too, but she didn't want to jump into a serious relationship. She'd married young, and she was in the process of divorcing her first husband. Now she was happy to be single and starting a teaching job in September. And finally, she really didn't want to get involved with a politician.

If Jill had paid more attention to Delaware politics, she might have realized how persistent Joe Biden could be. She might have guessed that he had great faith in his own judgment, and that he wouldn't let her go just because she had other plans for her life.

But for now, they compromised. Jill agreed that she wouldn't date anyone except him, and Joe seemed to accept that this wasn't a long-term commitment. After all, he did have two young children. And he wasn't about to give up politics.

However, Jill and Joe kept on spending time with

each other. Jill met Beau and Hunter, and sometimes the four of them went out together. Eventually, as she said later, "It felt like I dated three guys."

Joe met Jill's family and quickly felt at home with them. Even more so, Jill felt at home with Joe's family. After a few months, she was eating dinner most nights at the Station with Valerie and Jack and the boys, whether Joe was in town or not.

For Thanksgiving 1975, Jill suggested that she and Joe and the boys should go away for the weekend. They decided on Nantucket, an island off the coast of Massachusetts, for their getaway. During the long drive north, Jill helped Beau and Hunter make out their Christmas lists.

By the next year Joe, and especially Jill, still weren't sure they wanted to make a commitment. But Joe's sons had decided. They came to see their dad early one morning in 1976, while he was shaving. Joe could tell they were nervous, but determined, about something serious. Beau, seven years old, said to his brother, "You tell him, Hunt."

"No, you tell him," said six-year-old Hunter. There was a pause. Then he blurted out, "Beau thinks we should get married."

"We think we should marry Jill," added Beau.

Joe only said, "I think that's a pretty good idea." But inside, he was happier than he'd been for years. The only question was, would Jill agree? The next chance he got, he asked Jill to marry him.

At that time, Jill wouldn't say yes. She was all too aware that if she married Joe, she'd be "marrying" his sons, too. She loved the boys so much that she was afraid of letting them down. "I really had to make sure it was going to work," she explained later, "because I could not break their hearts if it didn't work."

And Jill was also more aware than ever that if she married Joe, she'd be marrying into Senator Biden's political life. She did not want to become a public person.

In 1976, President Ford was naturally the Republican candidate. Joe was eager to help the Democrats take back the White House in November. He believed that Jimmy Carter, former governor of Georgia, was the right candidate to unseat Gerald Ford. Biden was impressed by Carter's victories in the early primary elections, and he heartily approved of Carter's stand against racial segregation.

Joe Biden was the first senator to endorse Jimmy Carter, months before it was clear that Carter would win the Democratic nomination. Carter asked Biden to help him campaign, and Biden chaired his campaign steering committee. Biden traveled around the country to speak at rallies, urging audiences to turn out in November for Jimmy Carter. He sometimes joked that he'd been chosen to campaign because at age thirty-three, he was the only senator too young to run for president himself.

Publicly, Joe Biden didn't admit that he intended to run for president in the future. On a visit to his old grade school, Holy Rosary in Claymont, Senator Biden told the class that he was happy in his work as a senator. He had no ambitions, he assured them, to become president.

"You know that's not true, Joey Biden," said one of the nuns, waving a piece of lined paper. It was the essay he'd written about wanting to grow up to be president. She'd actually saved young Joey's paper for almost twenty years. So she had written proof that he'd thought about becoming president ever since age twelve.

Jimmy Carter won the election in November, and he was inaugurated as president on January 20, 1977. Meanwhile, Joe Biden was moving ahead in his Senate career. He'd already gained his longed-for seat on the Senate Foreign Relations Committee in 1975.

And in February 1977 he was happy to be appointed to the Senate Judiciary Committee. On this committee, Biden hoped to work for civil rights and justice, and against crime. He'd also have the chance to approve or disapprove the president's appointments to important government positions, such as secretary of defense or justice of the Supreme Court.

But next year, 1978, Senator Biden's six-year term would be up. In order to accomplish all he envisioned, he'd have to run for reelection. The issue of school busing was hotter than ever in Delaware. On the Judiciary Committee, Biden found himself caught in the middle, between anti-busing segregationists like Senator Eastland, chair of the committee, and pro-busing liberals like Senator Ted Kennedy.

## The School Busing Dispute

The Supreme Court's landmark decision in *Brown v. Board of Education* in 1954 ruled that racially segregated schools were harmful to children and therefore unconstitutional. A few school districts responded by busing a number of white students to Black schools, and Black students to white schools. The city of Berkeley, California, voluntarily began a busing program that was successful. However, most school districts quietly did nothing to integrate. And where busing did begin, some white families protested or even sued the schools.

Charlotte, North Carolina, had a token busing program, but it did not actually achieve racial balance. In 1965 the National Association for the Advancement of Colored People (NAACP) took the school district to court on behalf of ten Black families. Finally, in 1971, the Supreme Court required Charlotte to revise its busing program. The city was then fairly successful, at least for some years, in integrating its public schools. And a study showed that after integration, educational achievement for all students improved.

Boston, Massachusetts, was likewise ordered in 1974 to begin busing to correct racially segregated schools. But white Boston parents reacted with months of protests and sometimes violence. Thousands of white parents withdrew their children from the public schools and sent them to private or parochial schools, and thousands of white families moved to the suburbs, out of the Boston school district.

Even Black leaders had mixed opinions on whether school busing was a good way to integrate education. In any case, during the 1990s, the courts decided that busing for integration was no longer necessary. School districts that had been ordered to integrate schools by busing were released from such plans.

By now Joe and Jill had been going out for about two years. Joe still wanted to marry Jill, but he thought it was time for her to say yes or no. He told her that he was leaving on a Senate trip to South Africa. By the time he returned, ten days later, he and his sons would need an answer.

Joe wanted to marry Jill so much that he was willing to give up his promising political career. He'd decided that if Jill agreed to become his wife and Beau and Hunter's mother, he would not run for reelection in 1978.

But when Joe came back from South Africa, Jill wouldn't let him make that sacrifice. "If I denied you your dream," she explained to him later, "I would not be marrying the man I fell in love with." She'd decided she wanted to marry Joe so much, she was willing to become a politician's wife.

Joe's brothers, Jimmy and Frank, took Jill out privately and warned her that Joe had even bigger political ambitions than she knew. Joe, with the backing of his whole family, intended that one day he would become the president of the United States. Jill listened, but she didn't take this information too seriously at the time.

On June 17, 1977, Jill Jacobs married Joe Biden at the United Nations Chapel in New York City. It was a Catholic ceremony. Beau and Hunter, ages eight and seven, stood beside the bride and groom at the altar. Compared with most Biden gatherings, the wedding was small, just family and close friends.

After the luncheon reception, Joe and Jill Biden—and their two sons—went off on their honeymoon. The four Bidens saw the Broadway musical *Annie* and ate hamburgers at Blimpie's restaurant. Back at their hotel, Joe and Jill let the boys choose between the two hotel rooms they'd reserved. As Beau told it years later, the boys picked the honeymoon suite for themselves.

More seriously, Beau said how lucky he felt that

Jill had come into their life. "Led by my mom as much as my dad, we rebuilt our family."

As for the boys' aunt Valerie, her commitment to mothering the boys for more than four years was now complete. She and her husband, Jack Owens, moved out of the Station to a house of their own.

Chapter 9

# "We Rebuilt Our Family"

"Independent almost to a fault," President Jimmy Carter called Joe Biden. Biden had helped Carter win the presidency, and now President Carter was expected to help Senator Biden win reelection in 1978. And Carter did fly into Wilmington by helicopter in November 1977, and appeared briefly at two fundraising events. But he was not that enthusiastic about Biden.

Joe Biden, for his part, was disappointed in President Carter. He'd worked hard for Carter's election in 1976, but now he criticized the president openly. He didn't think Carter knew how to work with Congress. And he disagreed with Carter about busing. President Carter, as well as the NAACP and other civil rights groups, believed that busing was necessary to break down racial segregation in the schools.

The Supreme Court had ruled in 1971 that school districts could use busing to achieve racial balance. More recently, federal courts had *ordered* New Castle County, Delaware, to bus students to achieve racial balance. Public-school busing was the big issue of the Senate campaign in Delaware. Joe Biden's position was that he disagreed with the court order, but he thought it must be obeyed.

Biden bluntly called busing "an asinine concept." At the same time, he didn't want to be associated with most opponents of busing, who simply wanted to maintain racial segregation. "I don't want to be mixed up with a George Wallace," Biden had complained to an interviewer. George Wallace, governor of Alabama, was famous for declaring, "I say segregation now, segregation tomorrow, segregation forever."

But Joe Biden's liberal colleagues in the Senate did accuse him of letting the "racists" get to him. The Judiciary Committee was divided between the liberals, including Mike Mansfield, and the die-hard segregationists, including Senator James Eastland of Mississippi, chair of the Judiciary Committee since 1957.

Biden was for racial integration, and he'd supported most of Senator Edward Brooke's efforts to achieve equality, such as the Equal Credit Opportunity Act of 1974. But he believed that public-school busing would only cause white parents to pull their children out of the public educational system because they feared their children would be bused to inferior schools. Even parents who believed in equal education for all were not willing to take a chance on their own children's future.

So Biden thought that busing was the wrong way to go about integration. He'd made this argument in his first campaign for the Senate. It would work much better, Biden thought, to fight racial discrimination with housing, job opportunities, and college education. However, in 1974, Biden did vote with the liberal senators to make sure federal courts retained their power to enforce school integration if necessary.

Back home in Wilmington, parents against school busing were even angrier with Joe Biden than his Senate colleagues were. They knew he'd cast the deciding vote in 1974, leaving the courts with the power over local school districts to require school busing. Joe feared that the citizens of Delaware would vote against him for not preventing school busing, and so did Biden's chief aide, Ted Kaufman. Joe's Republican opponent tried to use this point, calling Biden too liberal for Delaware. Joe was seriously afraid of losing this election.

Jill campaigned alongside him, beginning in the summer of 1977 with a huge picnic for Biden supporters. Thousands of them showed up, and they all wanted to meet Jill and tell her how wonderful Neilia had been. Jill could have felt threatened by the task of following in Neilia's footsteps, but she greeted everyone graciously. After all, she and Joe both believed that Neilia's spirit was blessing their marriage.

Valerie managed Joe's campaign the same way she'd done in 1972. Four thousand volunteers swarmed over the state of Delaware, knocking on doors for Joe Biden. As it turned out, Biden didn't need to have worried about losing. On the first Tuesday in November 1978, Senator Biden easily won reelection, 58 percent to 41.

Afterward, Biden thought that the voters had trusted him, even though he couldn't solve the busing problem, because he listened to them. He let them vent their anger. As he wrote later, "I instinctively understood that my most important duty was to be a target."

Biden did remarkably well in the elections of 1978 compared with some of his fellow Democratic senators. Partly because President Carter was unpopular, several of them were voted out. And in Mississippi, Senator James Eastland's racism finally caught up with him.

The African Americans of Mississippi had gained voting rights and organized behind their Independent candidate, Charles Evers. The NAACP informed Eastland that they would not support him for reelection in 1978. Rather than lose, Eastland announced his retirement.

Meanwhile, at home in Wilmington, the Biden family continued to evolve. In spite of the fact that Beau and Hunter had advised their father to marry Jill, they didn't consider her their mother right away. After all, their aunt Valerie had mothered them for the last four-plus years, and so had their grandmother Jean. And before that, there had been their loving mother, Neilia, called "Mommy."

Jill was patient with Beau and Hunter, rather than trying to force intimacy. "I marveled at the way she let the boys come to her," Joe wrote later.

Jill volunteered at the boys' school. She did their laundry and cooked dinner every night. She kept the many pictures of Neilia displayed around the house for Beau and Hunter. And she regularly called the Hunter grandparents in upstate New York to let them know how the boys were doing.

At first Beau and Hunter called their new mother "Jill," as they had since Joe and Jill had started dating. And then, although no one asked them to, they began calling her "Mom." One day, when the boys were in the car, Jill stopped to refill the tank. Beau heard the gas station attendant ask, "How much gas do you want, hon?"

To Beau, about ten years old, "hon" sounded disrespectful. "Mom," he told Jill, "if he ever calls you 'hon' again, I'm going to go out there and say something to him."

In 1980, President Jimmy Carter ran for reelection. Usually, a president in office has a big advantage over a challenger, but Carter was in trouble with American voters. The economy was in a slump. Gasoline shortages caused long lines of unhappy drivers at gas stations. And to the shame of the nation, fifty-two

Americans were being held hostage in Iran.

In 1979, a popular revolution had swept the US-supported shah of Iran from power. That November, the revolutionaries had stormed the US embassy in the capital, Tehran, and captured the American staff. All during the 1980 campaign in the US, both Republicans and Democrats criticized President Carter for not freeing the hostages.

Senator Ted Kennedy ran for president in the Democratic primary elections against Carter. He was weighed down in the race by an old scandal from 1969, a car accident in which a young woman on his staff had drowned. However, Kennedy remained a candidate until the Democratic National Convention in August, and so the Democratic Party was weakened and divided.

In contrast, the Republican Party was united behind their candidate for president. Ronald Reagan, a former Hollywood actor and previous governor of California, projected a smooth, sunny personality. He promised to stimulate the economy by lowering taxes, to shrink the federal government, and to strengthen the US military. This conservative stance appealed to many voters in an uncertain time.

Joe Biden campaigned for Carter, but not

nearly as enthusiastically as he had in 1976. He, too, thought Carter was mismanaging the Iran hostage crisis. Representing the Senate Foreign Relations Committee, Biden and others traveled to the Persian Gulf in April 1980 to find out more about the hostages. The senators happened to be escorted by a naval officer named John McCain, who would become friends with Biden and later join him in the Senate.

Visiting an aircraft carrier in the Gulf, the senators accidentally discovered that the carrier held a fleet of large military helicopters. They immediately guessed that President Carter was about to launch a raid on the US embassy in Iran, to rescue the hostages. They were outraged that the Carter administration would undertake such a complicated, risky military action without even informing the Senate.

Soon afterward, Operation Eagle Claw, as the raid was called, was launched. It failed badly. The US Special Forces never even reached Tehran, and eight soldiers were killed.

In November 1980, Ronald Reagan won the presidency by a landslide. Reagan was almost seventy at his inauguration in 1981, the oldest man ever to become president. In his inaugural speech he expressed the way he intended to govern: "Government is not the solution to our problem; government is the problem."

## Reagan's Economics

Conservative Republicans believed that under Democratic presidents, the federal government had grown too big, costing taxpayers too much money to run. They also believed that federal agencies had too much power to regulate and tax businesses, which harmed the national economy. The solution, according to President Reagan and his supporters, was to cut taxes on wealthy investors and businesses, and to remove the regulations that were holding them back. They believed these policies would allow private businesses to thrive and automatically produce more wealth for everyone, including middle- and lower-class Americans.

But Democrats scornfully labeled the conservative war against taxes, especially taxes on big business and the wealthy, "trickle-down economics." They believed that government regulation was necessary, for instance, to prevent businesses from polluting the environment or taking unfair advantage of customers. And they believed the government did a better job than private businesses of providing certain services for all Americans. To do so, the government needed to collect taxes.

In the same election, Republicans won a majority of seats in the Senate. Biden's friend Ted Kennedy of Massachusetts had been chair of the Senate Judiciary Committee since 1978, but now he had to give way to Republican Strom Thurmond of South Carolina.

Senator Thurmond, elected to the Senate in 1954 as a Democrat, was a Dixiecrat who switched parties in 1964 to become a Republican. He was determined to use his powerful position as chair of the Judiciary Committee to fight against the Civil Rights Act of 1964, the Voting Rights Act of 1965, and the Civil Rights Act of 1968.

Even before Ronald Reagan's inauguration in early 1981, the Democratic Party began speculating about the 1984 campaign. Their candidate would have to begin organizing a team and raising money years ahead of the actual election. The party's eventual choice would be Walter Mondale, Jimmy Carter's vice president.

There was talk about Mondale picking the young senator from Delaware, Joe Biden, as his vice president, but Biden said he wouldn't accept that nomination. Some of Biden's advisors, including pollster Patrick Caddell, encouraged him to think of running for president himself. Biden was tempted. He'd turn forty-two in 1984, so he'd be old enough to be president. But after a long, serious talk with Jill, he decided not to register for the Democratic primary elections.

Biden felt that even if he had a good chance of winning this time, he wasn't ready. He wasn't sure he knew why he would run, or what he could accomplish if he was elected. As his good friend and advisor John Marttila had said, "You shouldn't run until you know the answers to those questions."

Besides, Joe thought a presidential campaign would be too much of a strain for his family. The Bidens had a brand-new member: in the summer of 1981, they welcomed a baby girl.

Beau and Hunter had actually found out about the baby coming before their father did. When Jill first thought she might be pregnant, she stopped at a pharmacy for a pregnancy test kit. The boys were with her in the car, and Jill explained to them why she was going into the pharmacy with a scarf covering her hair and wearing dark glasses. She wanted to keep the result of the test private, either way.

Beau and Hunter were excited to be the first ones in on the secret. Jill told them they could choose their baby sister's name, and they decided on "Ashley." And so Ashley Blazer Biden was born on June 8, 1981.

Earlier that year, in March, an assassin had shot and critically wounded President Reagan. Reagan recovered, but the attempt was a reminder, for anyone seeking the presidency, of that danger.

Joe Biden had plenty to keep him busy in the Senate. On the Judiciary Committee, he was eager to work on revising the US criminal code, which had not been updated since 1900. His double goal was to make the streets safe and to protect the civil rights of people accused of crimes. Black people, he knew, did not get treated fairly in the court system. On average, they got longer sentences for the same crime.

By the 1980s there was great concern about drug trafficking and the use of illegal drugs in the US. Several parts of the revisions of the US criminal code called the Comprehensive Crime Control Act of 1984 were written especially to try to correct this problem.

The conservatives in Congress, backed by President Reagan, thought the solution was to "get tough on crime." They wrote some harsh penalties, such as for possessing marijuana, that would turn out to do more harm than good.

Joe Biden was now the ranking member on the Judiciary Committee, and so he led the whole Senate in considering the Comprehensive Crime Control Act. In October 1984, President Reagan signed the act into law. At the time, Biden was proud of his work on this project. But many years later, he would see it as a mistake.

Meanwhile, he was again running for reelection to the Senate. By now he was firmly established in Delaware as a popular senator, and his campaign manager, Valerie, had campaigning down to a science. In November 1984, Biden won his third term by twenty percentage points. As for President Ronald Reagan, he won reelection by a second landslide, bigger than in 1980.

# Chapter 10

# "My Word as a Biden"

Why did Joe Biden want to be president? What would he do if elected? Those were the big questions.

By 1985, Biden felt more confident about his answers. The four years of President Reagan's first term had made clear to Biden how a Democratic president, and Biden in particular, could make a difference. He felt that Ronald Reagan's genial manner was only a front for the Republicans' stingy policies.

Republicans were cutting spending for welfare programs that the Democrats had put in place, such as Medicaid, food stamps, and public housing. The Republicans froze the minimum wage at $3.35 per hour and cut funding for federal education programs. As a result, the gap between the richest and the poorest Americans widened. The homeless population grew as more Americans could not pay their rent or mortgages.

And Biden believed that he was ready to lead the country. He understood working-class and middle-class Americans. And he'd served on the Senate Foreign Relations Committee for ten years, traveling outside the US and meeting leaders of foreign countries. "I knew the world and America's place in it in a way that few politicians did," he wrote later.

Joe Biden began making public appearances around the country, getting a sense of whether he had a realistic chance of winning the presidency in 1988. At least he would not be running against the immensely popular President Reagan, since Reagan was in his second and final term. Jill often went with Joe on these testing-the-waters trips, and so did Beau, sixteen, and Hunter, fifteen.

The boys were now both at Archmere Academy, their father's old high school. Beau would even be elected student body president with Hunter's campaign help. Unlike Joe, Beau was coolheaded and disciplined—in fact, his friends called him "the Sheriff." Hunter was the impulsive one. Both boys would do anything for each other, and anything for their father.

At the Iowa Democratic Party's dinner in November 1985, Biden presented himself as a young, vigorous senator like John F. Kennedy in 1960. He even used a phrase from Kennedy's presidential campaign, "Let's get America moving again." Biden sounded like a candidate, but he denied that he was planning to run for president in 1988. He didn't want to declare too early. First he wanted to be sure he'd have enough backing for the expensive, grueling campaign.

Jill was seriously worried about how a campaign for the presidency might strain their family. She'd talked to Lee Hart, the wife of Gary Hart, candidate for president in 1984. "It's harder than you can ever believe," Lee had told her. Although Jill and the children were well adjusted to being a senator's family, being a presidential candidate's family would be a much higher level of stress.

But Joe reassured Jill that he wasn't committing himself to actually running in 1988. He was only getting himself known around the country, demonstrating that he could appeal to audiences of voters. He was making connections with people who could donate money and help him campaign if he did run.

Besides, Joe Biden was still first and foremost a

father. Ashley, only four years old in 1985, was getting the same devoted treatment that Joe had lavished on Beau and Hunter when they were little. Years later, Ashley remembered him as always being around, even though he worked in Washington.

"I talked to him two times a day by phone," Ashley told Biden's biographer Jules Witcover. "He was always home at night, most of the nights, to catch dinner and to tuck us into bed." Biden still had the same rule about phone calls too: "If us kids called, that was it." No matter how important a meeting was, Biden's staff knew to get him out of it for a phone call from one of his children.

One thing in Washington that Biden wanted to change, if he did run, and if he was elected, was the Reagan administration's policy toward the white government of South Africa. The Black majority were struggling against oppression by the white minority, under a harsh segregation system called "apartheid." In the US, there was a strong movement to punish the government of South Africa with economic sanctions.

But President Reagan and his secretary of state, George Shultz, preferred a policy of "constructive engagement" with South Africa's white government. During a Senate Foreign Relations Committee hearing in 1986, Biden reproached Secretary Shultz for not coming down harder on South Africa. "I'm ashamed of the lack of moral backbone to this policy."

Some criticized Biden for this dramatic speech, in which he actually waved his fist at Secretary of State Shultz. They saw it as grandstanding, putting on a performance for the media audience rather than talking to Shultz. But Biden refused to be embarrassed. He told reporters, "There are certain things worth getting mad about."

By January 1987, Joe Biden had a good feeling about his chances in the 1988 presidential race. He was on the point of publicly announcing that he was running for president. But one problem he'd ignored up until now was that he didn't have a good relationship with the national media.

In a way this was odd, for someone as friendly and social as Biden. But during his first years in the Senate, when he was suffering grief over Neilia's death, he'd avoided talking to the press as much as possible. Even after that period, he still dashed for the train at the end of the day, anxious to get home to Beau and Hunter. Other politicians, staying around to have a cup of coffee or dinner with the reporters who covered the

Capitol, made valuable personal connections.

As a result, Biden's image with the national media was almost a cartoon: a tall guy with a great smile and a flair for connecting with an audience, but not much else. Joe Biden looked like a senator, and he talked like a senator—in fact, he had a reputation for talking on and on. But was there anything behind the image?

As one reporter put it, was Biden "more of a show horse than a work horse"? His fellow senators knew how hard he worked, but the national reporters might not dig up that information. However, Joe was confident that at least his character—his honesty, his "word as a Biden"—could not be attacked.

These days he had another problem to ignore: headaches. He'd never had headaches before this year, but by early 1987 he often felt as if his head were in a vise. He gulped extra-strength Tylenol, sometimes ten a day, as he flew from California to Iowa to Alabama to give speeches and shake hands. During one appearance in New Hampshire in March, Biden's pain was so severe that he had to duck backstage, retching. He barely managed to finish that speech.

At another event, he lost his temper at a questioner in the audience. That day Biden was not only suffering from splitting headaches but was also coming down with the flu. He thought the questioner was doubting his intelligence, and he went into a rant about his IQ and his outstanding record in college and law school. He hardly knew what he was saying. Afterward, he realized he'd exaggerated quite a bit.

This same year, Biden's duties in the Senate were heavier than ever. In January he'd become chair of the Senate Judiciary Committee. He knew that the Reagan administration was hoping to appoint a conservative judge to the Supreme Court. There were several older justices on the court who might retire or die, giving the president the chance to replace them. The question was, could Joe Biden do his vital work as a senator and run for president of the United States at the same time?

Even more important, as Jill pointed out, could Joe be the devoted husband and father he wanted to be? Could he still show up for family birthdays or school plays? She felt their life was perfect now the way it was. Beau would graduate from Archmere that spring, with Hunter only a year behind. Ashley was starting elementary school.

And although Joe didn't want to admit it, the headaches wouldn't go away.

Joe Biden carefully scheduled his announcement to avoid Beau's graduation from Archmere and Jill's and Ashley's birthdays. On June 9, 1987, in a dramatic stunt, Biden told a cheering crowd at the Wilmington train station that he was indeed running for president. Then he and his whole family rode a chartered train to Washington.

That same day in Scranton, Pennsylvania, the *Scranton Tribune*'s proud front-page story was all about Senator Joseph R. Biden and his bid for the presidency. And they'd dug up and reprinted the old photograph of young Joey Biden watching former president Truman in the Saint Patrick's Day parade.

Joe Biden was smart and talented, he had a great team behind him, and he had incredible reserves of energy. He'd always been confident that he could do anything, if he only kept working hard enough. However, running for president is a full-time job, and Biden couldn't ignore his duties as chair of the Senate Judiciary Committee. Shortly after his dramatic announcement, an opening came up on the Supreme Court. President Reagan's choice for the new justice was the ultraconservative Republican Robert Bork.

# The Supreme Court

The nine justices of the Supreme Court, plus the lower federal courts, make up the third branch of the US government, the *judicial* branch. These judges are appointed by the president (the *executive* branch) but must be confirmed by the Senate (the *legislative* branch, together with the House of Representatives). The Supreme Court has the power to review a law of the land, and to rule it either constitutional or unconstitutional—that is, to affirm a law, or to strike it down.

Since the founding of the United States, the Supreme Court has made some momentous decisions for the country. The *Dred Scott v. Sandford* decision in 1857 ruled that a slave could not become free even by escaping to one of the states where slavery had been abolished, and that even free African Americans were not entitled to the rights and privileges of citizens. The *Gideon v. Wainwright* decision in 1963 ruled that a person accused of a crime, if not able to pay for a lawyer to defend them, must be provided with one. In the *United States v. Nixon* case in 1974, the court ruled that the president is not above the law, and so President Nixon had to turn over recordings made in the Oval Office.

Supreme Court justices are appointed for life, so their influence can last much longer than that of the president or other elected officials. And a justice doesn't necessarily make decisions the way the president would like. The Republican president Dwight Eisenhower, who appointed Earl Warren as chief justice in 1953, later said that was one of his major mistakes. Eisenhower expected Warren to uphold conservative policies, but instead Warren led the court in making forceful decisions to outlaw racial segregation.

Up until now, the court had been fairly evenly balanced between liberal and conservative. But Judge Bork, if confirmed by the Senate, would push the Supreme Court over the line from moderate to conservative and back up the tendency of the Reagan administration to restrict civil rights and civil liberties. Bork had opposed the landmark Civil Rights Act of 1964. He had stated openly that he wanted to roll back Supreme Court decisions such as *Griswold v.*

*Connecticut*, which gave married couples the right to buy and use contraceptives.

Joe Biden had no doubt that Judge Bork would change the Supreme Court for the worse. But as chair of the Judiciary Committee, he was determined to give Bork a fair investigation. There was already an uproar of unfavorable publicity about Robert Bork's nomination. He was opposed by the American Civil Liberties Union, an organization that defends citizens' rights. He was also attacked for carrying out President Nixon's orders in 1973 during the Watergate scandal, which eventually led to Nixon's resignation from the presidency.

A fair investigation of Bork would take time and hard work, cutting into Biden's plans for his presidential campaign. And all the while his headaches were still plaguing him, in spite of the extra-strength Tylenol pills he kept taking. As Biden tried to protect civil rights and at the same time give Judge Bork a fair hearing, many accused him of being a weak leader. One columnist, George Will, called Biden "the incredible shrinking candidate."

In August 1987, as Biden worked to get the Senate Judiciary Committee ready to hold hearings on Robert Bork, the campaign for president was heating up. Biden needed to pay more attention to Iowa, the first state to vote in the primary season. Jill had already traveled there several times to campaign for her husband.

Now Biden needed to appear in Iowa himself. On August 23 there would be a debate among the Democratic candidates, the most important campaign event of the entire summer. Busy with preparing for the Bork hearings, Biden didn't take time to work on his debate speech. He trusted his ability to speak impromptu, and his gift for creating a bond with his audience.

During the plane trip to Iowa, Biden did ask one of his speechwriters how he should close the speech, since the closing makes the biggest impression. He decided to quote the words of a British politician, Neil Kinnock. Kinnock, campaigning for prime minister, had spoken eloquently about growing up in coal mining country, and being the first of his family to go to university.

Biden identified with Kinnock's passion for his background. Biden, like Kinnock, had grown up in coal mining country. He also came from people who were intelligent but never had a chance to go to college. As Kinnock put it, "There was no platform upon which they could stand."

These words, Joe Biden felt, expressed what the Democratic Party needed to do in the United States. The Republicans had knocked down the *platform* of government support built by Presidents Franklin Roosevelt and Lyndon Johnson for the working class. Democrats needed to be the party that rebuilt the platform better than ever. Biden had used this idea in speeches before, and it came naturally to him.

When it was Biden's turn to give his closing speech at the debate, he spoke Kinnock's words so movingly that some people in the audience wiped away tears. Afterward, one of his staff remarked that this time Biden had forgotten to give Kinnock credit, although he always had before. But it didn't seem like a big worry at the time.

Then, on Saturday, September 12, a story broke in both the *New York Times* and the *Des Moines Register*. The *Times* story, on the front page, said that Biden had "lifted Mr. Kinnock's closing speech." And quickly NBC News ran a split-screen video matching Biden's exact words with Kinnock's exact words. It made Joe's stomach hurt to watch it.

It seemed that the campaign manager of one of Biden's Democratic opponents, Michael Dukakis, had tipped off reporters about Biden's slip. Soon there was a chorus accusing Biden of plagiarism—using someone else's words as if they were his own. The media dug up another instance: at the California Democratic Convention in January, Biden had given a speech that included some words of Robert Kennedy's from twenty years before. A speechwriter had put the phrase in without telling Biden where it came from.

The media—"the sharks," as Ted Kaufman, now Biden's chief of staff, called them—had gone into a feeding frenzy. For more than a week the accusations of plagiarism grew louder, as Biden and his team tried to ignore them. A columnist in the *New York Times* called him "Plagiarizing Joe."

Jill was even more upset than Joe was. "Of all the things to attack you on. Your integrity?"

Meanwhile, even before the Judiciary Committee hearings on Robert Bork began, Senator Ted Kennedy gave an impassioned speech on the Senate floor against Bork. Biden loved and admired Kennedy, but this was just what he'd been afraid of. Kennedy, as well as other Democrats, was giving the public the impression that the Democrats on the committee had already made up their minds to block Judge Bork's appointment.

On Tuesday, September 15, Chairman Joe Biden

opened the Bork hearings in the Russell Senate Caucus Room. The hearings got off to a good start, and Biden felt confident that the Democrats could make a good case for rejecting Bork.

Then reporters dug up a mistake Biden had made twenty-two years before. It was his carelessness, back in his first year of law school, when he'd failed a technical writing course. He'd turned in a paper without giving proper credit to a source. Of course Biden's law school professors hadn't thought he was trying to cheat, but the media didn't care about that. What they cared about was making a good story, the story of Joe the Plagiarizer, even better.

And what Biden cared about, more than his campaign for president, was the damage the story might do to the so-important Bork hearings. At a private meeting, he asked the Judiciary Committee to choose another member as chair. "Absolutely not," said Republican Strom Thurmond. "This is ridiculous," said Ted Kennedy. Joe was deeply touched that his fellow senators had confidence in him, and he went on with the hearings.

But in the following days, the story in the media grew and grew: Biden was a plagiarizer, a liar, a blowhard, an empty suit. A news helicopter hovered over the Biden home, the Station, and reporters camped out near the house. Ashley, only six years old, had to go off to school in the mornings being filmed by TV cameras.

Finally, on the evening of September 22, Joe Biden called a council at the Station to decide what to do. The trusted inner circle in the living room included Jill, Beau, and Hunter; Joe's mother and father; his sister, Valerie, and her husband, Jack; and Joe's brothers, Jimmy and Frank. Biden's chief of staff, Ted Kaufman, and a few other trusted advisors were also there to help.

As Joe paced the living room, the discussion went back and forth. Beau, now a freshman at the University of Pennsylvania, and Hunter, a senior at Archmere, knew how much "My word as a Biden" meant to their father. They urged him to defend his honor on the campaign trail. But Joe had also given his "word as a Biden" to do his sworn duty as senator and chair of the Judiciary Committee.

Biden was torn. At one point during the evening, he stopped pacing and asked his mother, Jean, what she thought. She answered, "I think it's time to get out."

The next day, during a break in the Senate

Judiciary Committee hearings on Judge Bork, Biden stepped outside for a press announcement. With Jill at his side, he told the gathered journalists that he was dropping out of the race for president. He was angry that he had to make the choice, but he believed it was more important for him "to keep the Supreme Court from moving in a direction that I believe to be truly harmful."

Joe's sons were angry for him too. After he'd quit the race for the presidency, the three of them went to a football game at the University of Pennsylvania. One of the crowd recognized Senator Biden and started a chant about "Plagiarizing Joe." Hunter went after the heckler with his fists, and Joe and Beau had to restrain him.

At the end of the hearings in October, the full Senate voted not to confirm Bork, 58–42. A few months later President Reagan filled the empty seat on the Supreme Court with Anthony Kennedy, who would turn out to be a moderate influence. But bitter feelings toward the Democrats, on the part of Judge Bork and his Republican supporters, remained for many years.

Joe Biden was now free from the stress of campaigning for president. His family was out of the glaring spotlight, and the pressure from the Bork hearings was gone. Still, his headaches continued to plague him. One day near the beginning of 1988, while working out in the Senate gym, Biden felt a stab of pain in his neck. He left the gym and boarded the train to Wilmington as usual. But now, besides the pain in his neck, he felt numb on his right side, and his legs felt heavy.

These were signs of something very wrong. But Biden shook them off. He was determined to show the world that Joe Biden was not a quitter. As his father had always said, "If you get knocked down, get up." The next day, Biden saw a doctor, got a neck brace, and went on with his schedule of meetings, travel, and speeches.

But on the night of February 9, in a motel room in Rochester, New York, Joe Biden was struck down. He felt "something like lightning flashing inside my head, a powerful electrical surge—and then a rip of pain like I'd never felt before."

The next morning he was found lying on the floor of his room. He was rushed back to Wilmington. At Saint Francis Hospital, a spinal tap determined that Joe had suffered an aneurysm—a leakage of blood— inside his skull. He was given the last rites—prayers and blessing for the dying—by a Catholic priest.

The only hope for Joe was a dangerous and delicate operation, which had to be performed at the Walter Reed Army Medical Center near Washington. There the brain surgeon explained that a possible side effect of the surgery could be loss of speech. Biden joked, "I kind of wish that had happened last summer," meaning the fateful speech in which he'd forgotten to credit Kinnock's words.

The seven-hour surgery was successful. Joe's shaved, stitched head looked, as he wrote later, "like a misshapen baseball that had just had its cover nearly knocked off." But he was alive, and he could still speak.

Recovery, however, was slow and frustrating. At home a few weeks later, Biden suffered a blood clot in his lung and was taken back to Walter Reed Hospital for more treatment and medication. Finally leaving the hospital again, he had a defiant joke ready for the reporters waiting in the parking garage: "I've decided to announce that I am reentering the race for president."

The reality was that for the first time in his life, Joe Biden was forced to slow down. No visitors. No work, even from home. No phone calls, even from the president. He slept a great deal, and gradually he healed. In May he returned to the hospital for surgery on another aneurysm, and stayed there for several more weeks. Then back home for a whole summer of just rest and recovery.

The experience of nearly dying, and then having to live life in the slow lane for months on end, made Joe Biden look at life differently. He didn't feel the same pressure to succeed at everything, every time. His campaign for president had come to a humiliating close, but that wasn't the end of the story of Joe Biden.

He was still a senator, still chair of the Foreign Relations Committee and the Judiciary Committee. After Labor Day he was finally able to board the Amtrak train to Washington again. In the Senate Chamber, Biden's colleagues gave him a standing ovation.

Chapter 11

# Stand Up to Bullies

Beau and Hunter Biden were worried about their father. The night Joe Biden had decided to drop out of the presidential race of 1988, they'd pleaded with him to keep fighting. If Joe gave up this fight, they feared, he would also drop out of public life — his chosen life's work. "But, Dad," Beau said, "if you leave, you'll never be the same."

In fact, Joe Biden did not give up his plan of running for president. He only decided to be patient, rebuild his political reputation, and wait for the right time. For now, as he settled back into his work in the Senate, he could enjoy his family.

In September 1988, Hunter Biden entered Georgetown University in Washington, DC. He worked at the school to help pay for his room and board, as Beau did at the University of Pennsylvania, and took out a student loan. As Joe Biden liked to remind voters, he was a middle-class citizen, like most of them. The Senate was full of millionaires, but Joe Biden wasn't one of them.

That fall, the race for president was in the final stages. Mike Dukakis of Massachusetts had won the Democratic nomination, but President Reagan's vice president, Republican George H. W. Bush, won the general election on November 8. Now the Republicans would have four more years to nominate conservatives to the Supreme Court.

Meanwhile, Joe Biden's top concern in Congress was working on a bill called the Violence Against Women Act. Biden had been working on crime issues in the Senate since his first term, but he was shocked and disgusted to learn how widespread violence against women was in the US. Too many married men beat and sometimes killed their wives. Too many young men abused the women they dated.

Biden had been raised to believe that for someone in a position of power, the worst sin was to abuse that power. He often brought this up with his children during dinner-table discussions, and it made a deep impression on Ashley. In elementary school, she wrote an essay on what she wanted to be when she grew up: she wanted to help abused women. And she would, in fact, become a social worker.

Abuses of power came up in foreign relations too. In the Middle East, trouble arose between Iraq, ruled by the dictator Saddam Hussein, and its neighboring countries. On August 2, 1990, Iraq invaded and quickly defeated Kuwait. The Bush administration was concerned that Saudi Arabia, a US ally and an important source of oil, would be attacked next, and President Bush began to build up US forces.

Biden agreed with President Bush that Iraq's aggression had to be stopped. But as chair of the Senate Foreign Relations Committee, he questioned whether US interests in the Middle East justified going to war. Joe Biden had begun his political career campaigning against the "quagmire" of the Vietnam War. He feared that an attack on Iraq could turn into another such costly and useless mission.

Biden also insisted, as chair of the Senate Judiciary Committee, that the president needed to consult with Congress before he sent American troops into battle. According to the Constitution of the United States, the president is the commander in chief of the armed forces. But only Congress has the power to declare war on another country.

However, without much consulting, President Bush pushed a resolution through the United Nations Security Council. Biden voted against it, but the majority of the Senate voted to approve it. On January 17, 1991, the US, the United Kingdom (UK), and other allies attacked Iraq. In a matter of weeks, Kuwait was liberated and Iraq was defeated. The American public overwhelmingly approved of such a swift and successful military action.

That summer, on June 27, Supreme Court Justice Thurgood Marshall announced his retirement at the age of eighty-two. He was the first and the only African American on the court. President Bush was determined to replace him with a reliably conservative judge.

To the surprise of Joe Biden, the rest of the Judiciary Committee, and many others, Bush's choice was Clarence Thomas. Thomas, a judge in the federal court system, did not have nearly the experience and prestige of Judge Robert Bork, or even of most candidates for the Supreme Court. But he was very conservative, and he was Black.

The Senate Judiciary Committee, chaired by Joe Biden, was in a bind. If Judge Thomas had been white, it would have been easy to reject him because of his lackluster record. However, if the committee rejected an African American nominee, they could be accused of racial bias. Even more than with Robert Bork, Biden was anxious to run the committee's hearings in a way that was absolutely fair.

Leading the questioning of Thomas, Biden's plan was to expose him as so stubbornly conservative that he would not be able to judge a case fairly. Biden was sure Thomas had already made up his mind about issues likely to come before the Supreme Court, especially about a woman's right to choose whether or not to bear a child. But Thomas refused to state his position on that issue.

As senators continued to question him, Thomas even insisted that he had no opinion on the issue one way or the other. This was hard to believe. But Thomas would not be pinned down and give the committee a chance to reject him.

Then the Judiciary Committee learned of an entirely different reason why they should consider rejecting Clarence Thomas. Anita Hill, a law professor who used to work for Judge Thomas, accused him of a pattern of sexual harassment. If Hill was telling the truth, Thomas had abused his power as her employer, and he was not worthy to be seated on the highest court in the land.

Biden wasn't sure what to do. Clarence Thomas's nomination was already a high-profile news story. Anita Hill's accusations could make it "a giant incendiary bomb," as he said later.

Anita Hill did not want to be publicly involved in the hearings, but in the end, she came and testified before the committee. Clarence Thomas denied all her accusations. Furthermore, he angrily accused the Senate Judiciary Committee of racial bias for even allowing Hill's testimony. He called the hearings "a high-tech lynching for uppity Blacks."

The committee decided to make no recommendation to approve or disapprove. On October 15, 1991, the full Senate narrowly confirmed Thomas as the new justice on the Supreme Court.

As for Judiciary chair Joe Biden, he had lingering bad feelings about these hearings. Against his will, they had turned from hearings into a trial of Clarence Thomas, and then into a trial of Anita Hill. He was afraid that Anita Hill's supporters thought he had allowed her to be unfairly humiliated and dismissed.

Biden was also afraid that Thomas's supporters would accuse him of racial bias. He talked and talked, during and after the hearings, trying to assure all sides that he was doing his best to be fair. Many simply thought he was talking too much.

While the Clarence Thomas hearings had dragged on, Joe Biden had been hearing alarming reports from Yugoslavia in eastern Europe. Biden had made many trips to the region for the Senate Foreign Relations Committee, and he knew more than most senators about Yugoslavia. The country was an ethnic mix, and the Serbian majority was abusing the Muslim and Roman Catholic minorities. But in 1991 the Bush administration was mainly concerned that the country was breaking apart. To help keep Yugoslavia together, they supported the Serb leader Slobodan Milosevic as the president.

By August 1992, civil war was raging in the former Yugoslavia. Bosnia, a section populated mainly by Muslims and Croats, had tried to declare independence. Milosevic's artillery was pounding every city in Bosnia. Worse, the Serbs were carrying out a policy of what they called "ethnic cleansing"—actually, murdering or driving out all the non-Serbs in Bosnia.

In fact, Milosevic was committing genocide, trying to destroy a whole ethnic group. The next year, traveling to Yugoslavia to meet Milosevic, Biden would not shake his hand or sit down to a meal with him. He told the Serb leader to his face, "I think you're a damned war criminal."

While Joe Biden was more and more worried about the horrifying crimes being committed in Bosnia, most of the US was focused on the presidential election of 1992. Reporters had asked Biden if he was thinking of running this time, but he wasn't. In the previous four years, he'd almost died from the aneurysms, and he'd led the Judiciary Committee through two of the most difficult Supreme Court nominations in the history of the US. And he'd tried hard—and failed—to push his Violence Against Women Act through Congress.

As it happened, Democrat Bill Clinton defeated Republican president George H. W. Bush in November 1992. At the time, the Democratic Party had a reputation of being "soft on crime," and Clinton promised that his administration would act to control crime. Joe Biden worked hard with others in Congress to write the Violent Crime Control and Law Enforcement Act. His Violence Against Women Act was part of this sweeping crime control bill. So was a ban on assault weapons, the military-grade guns used in mass shootings.

In 1994, President Clinton signed the bill. Biden was proud of his accomplishment, and he was widely praised at the time, by the police as well as women's groups. Unfortunately, the Violence Against Women Act would be weakened later by the Supreme Court. And the assault weapons ban was allowed to expire in ten years.

But worse, the bill would turn out to have unintended consequences. It included harsher sentences, including the death penalty, for many crimes. More people were imprisoned for longer times, and the populations in state and federal prisons grew.

In the Biden family, Beau and Hunter were pursuing their adult lives. Beau, like his father, attended the Syracuse University law school, with the intention of going into politics. Hunter spent a year as a volunteer in Oregon, where he met and married Kathleen Buhle in 1993. Later that year, Joe's first grandchild was born. Hunter named her Naomi, after his lost sister.

In 1996, Senator Joe Biden was up for reelection again. Hunter was now living in Wilmington with his wife and little daughter, and Joe appointed him as his deputy campaign manager. Deputy, of course, to Aunt Valerie, who was still running Joe's campaigns. Hunter also had a job with Maryland Bank, N.A. (MBNA).

Joe Biden hadn't given up the idea of running for president, but 1996 was not the right time either. President Bill Clinton was naturally the Democratic nominee, and he was reelected.

The next year, 1997, Hunter bought his own house in Wilmington and opened it, as Joe always had, to friends and family. Beau moved into the third floor. He was now working as a prosecutor for the US Attorney's Office in Philadelphia. He met his future wife, Hallie Olivere, at one of the gatherings at Hunter's house.

Toward the end of 1998, Hunter left his job at MBNA in Wilmington and took a position in President Clinton's administration. He and Kathleen moved to Washington, DC, where their daughter Naomi would attend the Sidwell Friends School. Their second daughter, Finnegan, was born in 1998, and a third daughter, Maisy, in 2000. As for Joe and Jill, they had become "Pop" and "Nana."

In the presidential campaign of 2000, Al Gore,

Clinton's vice president, ran against the Republican candidate, Governor George W. Bush of Texas. That November, the election results were too close to call. Weeks later, the election was decided by another close vote, 5–4, by the Supreme Court. There was a conservative majority on the court, and they ruled in favor of Bush. This was yet another example of how important appointments to the Supreme Court had become.

Hunter was still in Washington with his family, but now he had a new job. He was a professional lobbyist, hired by businesses or other groups to try to influence public officials. He and his father had an unspoken agreement not to discuss Hunter's business. Since Senator Biden was a powerful political figure, they didn't want to give the impression that Joe was using his influence to help his son's business dealings.

On the morning of September 11, 2001, Senator Biden boarded the Amtrak train, as usual, at the Wilmington station. His train was halfway to Washington when Jill called him with stunning news: two planes had crashed into the World Trade Center towers in New York City. The country was under attack.

In Washington, Biden heard that a third plane had hit the Pentagon, the military headquarters of the

United States. Joe Biden's instinct was to run toward the Capitol. If we were under attack, he thought, the citizens of the United States would be terrified. He felt that Congress ought to reassure the country by staying in session as usual.

But security officers were herding people away from the government buildings, and Biden was not allowed to enter the Capitol. Ashley called as he was standing in the park across the street. "Daddy!" She'd heard on the news that a fourth plane was headed for Washington. "Get out of there!"

Several hours later, Joe Biden did get out of Washington, after trying in vain to persuade Congress to stay in session. But first he gave an interview to an ABC reporter, reassuring Americans that the government would stand strong and the country would pull through the crisis. During the drive home, Biden answered a call from President Bush, who had been spirited away from Washington on Air Force One by the Secret Service. He praised Biden's reassuring speech.

Beau Biden, like his father, had the instinct to run *toward* danger, to come to the defense of his country. In 2003 he joined the National Guard. The year before, he and Hallie had married. Their daughter, Natalie, was born in 2004, and their son, Robert Hunter Biden II (named after Hunter), in 2006.

Joe Biden liked and respected President George W. Bush, but Biden mistrusted the president's advisors, led by Vice President Dick Cheney. They seemed bent on invading Iraq, although it was a terrorist group called Al Qaeda, not Iraq that had attacked the US on September 11, 2001. To convince Congress to invade Iraq, the Bush administration claimed to have proven that Iraq had harbored Al Qaeda terrorists, and that Iraq now had weapons of mass destruction. At that, Senator Biden and most of his colleagues voted to give the president the power to invade Iraq. In 2003, the Bush administration launched what they promised would be a quick and easy military mission.

In the campaign for president in 2004, Biden's friend Senator John Kerry of Massachusetts was the Democratic candidate. Biden honestly thought that American voters would choose Kerry, a decorated combat veteran of the Vietnam War. Americans were unhappy about the Iraq War. The conflict had dragged on, costing nine hundred American lives and many billions of dollars so far.

But in November, Senator Kerry lost to President

Bush. However, in Illinois a young politician named Barack Obama won his election for senator. Joe Biden was impressed with Obama's intelligence, his work ethic, and his understanding of how the US fit in among the nations of the world. Biden promised to get Obama a seat on the Senate Foreign Relations Committee.

Now Joe Biden was determined to run for president in 2008. He was deeply disturbed by George W. Bush's choices in foreign policy, but even more disturbed by the division that was widening in American politics. There was less and less cooperation between Democrats and Republicans. Biden thought the Republican attacks on John Kerry had been especially nasty.

Biden believed that if he were president, he could bring together the hostile factions in Iraq and finally end that war. Jill, who had hung back from politics in the past, now wholeheartedly believed that he should run. In June 2005, Joe appeared on CBS's *Face the Nation* and stated frankly that he intended to run in 2008. He began to gather his campaign team.

As President George W. Bush's second term went on, the Iraq War looked more and more like a bad mistake. And in August 2005, Hurricane Katrina struck New Orleans, causing the worst national disaster in

US history. President Bush was widely criticized for mishandling the national response.

In 2006, the prices of housing collapsed, the first sign that the US economy was sliding toward the Great Recession of 2007–2008. With the congressional elections of 2006, the Democratic Party regained control of both the House of Representatives and the Senate. More than ever, Joe Biden was convinced that he should make a new run for the presidency.

Before launching a campaign for president, candidates often write a book to present themselves to the public. Joe Biden told his life story in *Promises to Keep*, published in 2007. The dedication page read, "For Mom and Dad, who kept their promises." While most political memoirs are bland and boring, Biden's book was highly readable. He told an inspiring personal story of challenges overcome, of love and tragedy and finding love again.

In January 2007, Joe Biden told *Meet the Press* that he was definitely running for president. This time, he declared, he was "going to try to be the best Biden I can be." He didn't mention a serious Biden family worry.

While the Bidens were proud that Beau had

just been elected attorney general of Delaware, his younger brother, Hunter, was struggling with addiction. Unlike his father, Hunter had started drinking in high school. In recent years he had been in and out of recovery programs.

Just days before Joe Biden announced his candidacy for the Democratic nomination, Hunter and his uncle Jimmy were in the headlines. They had gotten entangled in a risky high-finance deal and lost a large sum of money. Furthermore, a third business partner was suing them. This publicity was not good for Biden's campaign.

However, it was Joe himself, not his reckless son, who would undermine his chances for the Democratic nomination.

In the campaign of 2008 there were several Democratic candidates, but the two getting the most attention were Senator Hillary Clinton of New York, wife of former president Bill Clinton, and Senator Barack Obama of Illinois. Hillary Clinton was the first woman who seemed to have a good chance of being nominated. And Obama, an African American, was a rising young star in the Democratic Party.

Biden didn't think Obama was a strong candidate, because he'd been elected to the Senate only four years before. But he thought it spoke well of the Democratic Party that Obama was in the race. As he said to a reporter for the *New York Observer*, Obama was "the first mainstream African American who is articulate and bright and clean and a nice-looking guy."

*Oops.* Joe Biden had spoken without thinking. His careless words exploded into the media. In the *Wilmington News Journal*, the headline on February 1, 2007, was SEN. BIDEN STUMBLES OUT OF GATE IN '08 RACE.

Joe had not meant his remark the way it sounded, and he immediately called Barack Obama to apologize. Obama didn't take it personally, but it did make him think twice about Biden's judgment.

Biden and his campaign pressed on through 2007, but they had a hard time raising money. In November, in a Democratic debate on CNN, he was almost ignored by the moderator. However, Joe was sincerely enjoying campaigning. More than any other time he'd run for office, he felt he was being his authentic self.

As always, he had the full support of his family. Hunter was by his side, a "security blanket," as Hunter put it later, as Joe drove to Iowa for the caucuses. Joe and his team pinned their hopes on this first event of the primary contest. If Biden came in third, he'd have a solid footing to continue.

But the Iowa caucuses on January 3, 2008, wiped out Joe Biden's 2008 campaign for the presidency. He came in fifth. His chance at the Oval Office in the White House was gone — at least for this cycle.

Ashley Biden admired her father for the way he comforted his family. After all, he told them, he still had a job that he loved. He was going back to the Senate, where he could accomplish a lot for the country as chair of the Foreign Relations Committee.

Some people wondered if, when the Democratic primary elections were over, Biden might be picked for vice president. Biden had already answered that question, telling an interviewer in August 2007, "I can absolutely say with certainty I would not be anybody's vice president, period. End of story. I guarantee I will not do it."

## The Vice Presidency

Many presidents have chosen a vice president purely because they thought that person would help bring in voters on Election Day. As a result, many presidents did not even like the vice president they felt they had to choose. And some vice presidents have not been qualified for their main duty: to take over leadership of the country if the president dies or is disabled.

In the history of the United States, it has happened nine times that the vice president became president because the sitting president was unable to serve. Eight vice presidents have stepped into the Oval Office after the president's death. Gerald Ford became president when Richard Nixon resigned.

The Constitution gives the vice president only two other duties: to preside over the Senate, and to cast the deciding vote in the Senate in the case of a tie. "The most insignificant office that ever the invention of man contrived or his imagination conceived" was the disgusted way that John Adams, vice president to George Washington, described his position in 1789. And John Nance Garner, Franklin Roosevelt's first vice president, in 1933, had similar feelings, although he expressed them less eloquently: "The vice presidency isn't worth a bucket of warm piss."

However, during the twentieth century the

vice presidency grew to include advising the president, representing the president, and helping the president govern. Lyndon Johnson was invaluable to President Kennedy in working with Congress, and Walter Mondale brought foreign relations experience to President Jimmy Carter's team. George W. Bush's vice president, Dick Cheney, was criticized for taking on too much importance. He was accused of making policy decisions on his own, without the president's knowledge.

From January to June 2008, Senator Barack Obama of Illinois and Senator Hillary Clinton of New York fought for the Democratic nomination for president. Joe Biden would not endorse either one until the choice was final. But he promised to work hard, campaigning for the primary winner in the fall.

Barack Obama was already thinking carefully about who he'd want on his team if he were elected. Joe Biden would certainly be a good choice to balance the ticket. While Obama was a younger African American man from the middle class, Biden was an older white man with working-class roots.

Obama had been elected to the Senate only a few

years before. Biden, serving in the Senate for thirty-six years, had many connections in Congress and in foreign countries. And his outgoing, passionate style of campaigning complemented Obama's cool, reserved style.

Obama did want a candidate for vice president who could help him win the election. But he also wanted a person highly qualified for the job—and he wanted someone who would work well with him. He respected Joe Biden's achievements in the Senate, including his ability to get along with Republicans as well as Democrats. Obama also thought Biden's years of experience in foreign relations would be valuable.

In June, when Obama was sure of winning the Democratic nomination, he called Biden and asked if Joe wanted to be considered for vice president. Biden said no. He enjoyed his respected position as chair of the Senate Foreign Relations Committee, and he wasn't sure he wanted to trade that to become the president's sidekick. Obama insisted that he think some more about it. "Go home and talk it over with the family first."

To Joe's surprise, Jill thought that he should say yes. For one thing, she said, if the Bidens were living in the vice president's residence in Washington, they'd be right near Hunter and his family. And on weekends and vacations, they'd still have their house in Wilmington, right near Beau and his family.

Jean Biden, Joe's mother, agreed with Jill. Hadn't Joe always believed in the cause of civil rights? This was his chance to do something really important for civil rights. He could help elect the first African American president of the United States.

In the summer weeks leading up to the Democratic Convention, Barack Obama became pretty sure that Joe Biden was his first choice for vice president. One factor that impressed Obama was Biden's devotion to his family. Obama's aide David Axelrod noticed the Bidens' open affection for each other too. "There's something really special about that family," he told Obama.

Before Obama made his choice, Joe Biden met him privately, in a hotel in Minneapolis, for a final three-hour discussion. Biden explained that if he were Obama's vice president, he would want to be his chief advisor. "If you're going to ask me to do this, please don't ask me for any reason other than that you respect my judgment. If you're asking me to join you to help govern, and not just help you get elected, then I'm interested."

That meant that Biden would want to meet with the president in private at least once a week and be included in all important group meetings. Of course, final decisions would always be for the president to make, but Biden wanted to be consulted.

Obama, for his part, sincerely wanted a vice president who would tell him the truth, rather than what the vice president thought the president wanted to hear. Obama was convinced that Joe Biden would do just that. In fact, Biden was famous for saying what he thought, even when he should have kept his mouth shut.

The two men were on the same page.

# Chapter 12

# Mr. Vice President

On August 7, 2008, only weeks before the Democratic National Convention, Russian troops invaded the neighboring country of Georgia. The Bush administration condemned Russia's action. A cease-fire was brokered, but Russia still threatened the smaller, weaker country.

As chair of the Senate Foreign Relations Committee, Joe Biden flew to Tbilisi, the capital of Georgia. He met with the Georgian president, and he returned home recommending that the United States should send Georgia $1 billion in aid. Barack Obama recognized this moment as great publicity for Biden—and for his own campaign, if he chose Biden as vice president.

Two days before the Democratic Convention,

Obama called Biden to officially offer him the job. Biden took the call at a dentist's office, where Jill was undergoing a root canal procedure. Joe was so happy and excited that he started talking a mile a minute.

As Obama and Biden began campaigning together, the two men discovered things they had in common. They both loved sports, and they both understood how to be team players. They were both devoted to their families.

Their families hit it off too. "I liked Jill, Joe's wife, right away," Michelle Obama wrote later in her memoir, *Becoming*. Jill, like Michelle, had hesitated to commit to her husband's political career. Jill had also pursued a career while raising children.

"And then there were the Biden grandkids, five altogether, all of them as outgoing and unassuming as Joe and Jill themselves," Michelle remembered. Beau's Natalie and Robert, plus Hunter's Naomi, Finnegan, and Maisy, absorbed the Obamas' daughters into their noisy, excited bunch.

During the Democratic National Convention in late August, the Biden family was showcased. Beau, attorney general of Delaware, soon to be sent to Iraq with the National Guard, proudly introduced his father.

Joe Biden in turn proudly introduced Hunter, Ashley, and Jill, joking that his wife was "the only one who leaves me breathless and speechless at the same time." And as he talked to the audience about his family background, he introduced Jean Finnegan Biden, his ninety-one-year-old mother. Sadly, his father had not lived to see this moment.

That night at the convention, Joe's granddaughter Finnegan, ten years old, asked Joe if Malia and Sasha Obama, ten and seven, could sleep over with the Biden kids. Later that night, Biden checked the children's room in the Bidens' hotel suite. He was touched to see them all in their sleeping bags, "cuddled together." He felt sure he'd made the right decision in joining forces with the young senator from Illinois.

As they plunged into the final two months of the 2008 race, Obama appreciated Joe Biden's experience with political campaigns. Biden might have a reputation as a motormouth, but he was a skilled campaigner. Obama's staff were impressed that Biden could campaign in a disciplined way, keeping the spotlight on the candidate for president rather than on himself.

Biden launched his race for vice president with a trip to his childhood home in Scranton, Pennsylvania.

On Labor Day, Joe and his mother visited the old Finnegan house on North Washington Avenue, where a woman named Anne Kearns lived with her family. They were thrilled to welcome Senator and Jean Biden to a backyard picnic. As Joe toured the house, they urged him to sign the wall of the attic room where he used to sleep.

*I Am Home*, Biden wrote with a Sharpie. *Joe Biden, 9-1-08*. Then he joked, "If my father was here, he'd smack me for writing on the wall."

The Republican candidate for president was Senator John McCain of Arizona, a force on the Senate Armed Services Committee and a war hero to boot. He had served in the Senate with Joe Biden for more than twenty years. They were close friends, in spite of their political differences.

But that didn't mean that Biden would go easy on McCain. On the campaign trail, he hammered at the idea that a President McCain would be four more years of the unpopular George W. Bush. Under President Bush, the country was suffering the worst economic crisis since the Great Depression of the 1930s. People were losing their homes to risky mortgages, and as unemployment soared, people also lost their health insurance. But the government bailed out big banks, which enraged ordinary citizens.

McCain had chosen Sarah Palin, governor of Alaska, as his vice presidential candidate. At first this announcement gave McCain a bump upward in the polls. But by late September the Obama-Biden team had pulled ahead.

Obama and his campaign team had known from the beginning that Joe Biden talked too much. Back in 2005, when Obama attended his first Senate Foreign Relations Committee meeting, that was his main impression of Senator Biden. "Man, that guy can just talk and talk." Worse, maybe as a side effect of talking so much, Biden made gaffes—like the one about Obama being "clean" and "articulate."

So Obama expected that Joe would make some gaffes during the campaign, and that the media would be waiting to pounce on each one. That was part of the package of Joe Biden. As the campaign went on and Biden did put his foot into his mouth, and the media did jump on it, Obama treated each occasion as no big deal.

Until a fundraising event in October, when Joe, going off script, told the audience, "Mark my words. It will not be six months before the world tests Barack

Obama." This remark seemed to echo what Biden had said during the Democratic primary debates, suggesting that Obama wasn't "ready" to be president. (Of course, back in 1972, people in Delaware had wondered if a twenty-nine-year-old county councilman named Joe Biden was "ready" to be their senator.)

Biden was only speaking from his experience in foreign relations, where some crisis or other was always coming along. He meant that there was bound to be an international crisis at the beginning of Obama's presidency, and that the crisis would prove the new president's leadership.

However, the McCain campaign was delighted to quote—and misinterpret—Biden's unnecessary remark. They were already making the point that Obama was inexperienced in foreign policy, and Biden's words seemed to show that even Obama's running mate thought so. "How many times is Biden gonna say something stupid?" wondered Obama to his aides.

But by that time, Obama was ahead of McCain in the polls, and he stayed ahead up through Election Day, November 4. That historic evening, the Obamas and the Bidens were staying in the same hotel in Chicago, watching the election returns. At ten o'clock the TV networks announced the winner: Barack Obama. The Bidens burst into the Obamas' room, everyone yelling and hugging each other.

On the bright, cold day of January 20, 2009, Joe Biden stood on the steps of the Capitol. The crowds for the inauguration of Barack Obama, the first African American president, were the biggest ever, for any event in Washington, DC. Jill held the Biden family Bible while Joe took the oath of office as vice president of the United States. Hunter and Ashley stood by, beaming. So did Beau, on special leave from his National Guard assignment in Iraq.

Now Barack Obama was the forty-fourth president, the office Joe Biden had set out to win two years before. Biden was just as ambitious and confident as Obama, and he knew it would be hard for him, after his years of leadership in the Senate, to call someone else boss. But he didn't intend to be a vice president like the one before him.

During the 2008 campaign, Biden had called George W. Bush's vice president, Dick Cheney, "the most dangerous vice president we've had probably in American history." He meant that Cheney had taken too big and too independent a role in the Bush administration. Cheney had urged the president into aggressive military actions, ignored Congress, and brushed aside human rights concerns.

Joe Biden knew how to play on a team, and he surprised many people by putting his own ego aside to work with the new president. Just as when Coach Walsh at Archmere had chosen Mike Fay, instead of Joe, to be football captain, Biden accepted his position in second place. There was a lot to be done, and it could only be done with teamwork.

Between the election in November 2008 and the inauguration in January 2009, Obama had consulted with Biden about choosing his cabinet. One of the most important posts was secretary of state, and Barack and Joe agreed that he should ask Hillary Clinton. Obama agreed, in fact, with most of Biden's recommendations for members of the cabinet. "Not because I made them," Biden explained on ABC News, "but because we think a lot alike." The two men shared certain values, and they were also both practical thinkers.

The most urgent task for the new president and his team was to rescue the US economy from the Great Recession. In February 2009, Congress passed, and President Obama signed into law, a bill for $787 billion to stimulate the national economy. Obama gave Biden the responsibility of overseeing the handout of the money to states and cities, to infrastructure projects such as repairing bridges, and for direct assistance to individuals. Biden's special focus was to look after the middle class, which was not as well off as it used to be.

Also urgent was the war in Iraq. There were still 150,000 US troops in Iraq, and the war had already cost US taxpayers over $600 billion. President Obama had campaigned on the idea that the Iraq War, launched by President George W. Bush in 2003, was a "dumb war."

As the Obama administration got underway in 2009, the president asked Joe Biden to oversee his policy of withdrawing US troops from Iraq. Vice President Biden flew to Iraq in July 2009 to help with this transition, by meeting with Iraqi leaders and urging cooperation among the hostile factions in Iraq. On that same trip, Joe Biden also had a chance to hug Delaware National Guard captain Beau Biden, stationed in Iraq.

High on Obama and Biden's to-do list was a national health plan. Joe Biden had believed in the need for a national health care program since he first ran for senator in 1972. President Bill Clinton had attempted to reform US health care during his first term, but in 1994 the proposed plan had died in Congress.

## National Health Care

In 2009, almost all industrialized countries of the world had a national health insurance plan that guaranteed a basic level of care for the whole population. But the US had a patchwork system in which some Americans received health insurance through their employers and some bought private insurance. Some were covered by government programs such as Medicare, for those over sixty-five, or Medicaid, a state-run program for low-income people.

However, more than forty million Americans had no health insurance at all. Many of them had to decide between buying lifesaving medications, such as insulin for diabetes, and paying the rent. In 2013, the National Research Council and the Institute of Medicine showed that US citizens had a shorter life expectancy than people in most other wealthy nations, in spite of the fact that the US spent more on health care than any other nation in the world.

For years there had been efforts in the US, including the Clinton administration's failed plan, to set up a national health insurance system for all Americans. The main problem in achieving health care for everyone was that politicians disagreed about how much control the federal government should have. Some wanted the government to run the program, as it did Medicare. Others felt that private insurance companies could offer better services. And pharmaceutical companies fought any attempts to control the high prices of medications.

Joe Biden had good relations with many members of Congress. He felt hopeful that Congress could work out a health care reform bill fairly quickly. At first it seemed that the House of Representatives and the Senate would cooperate to craft a bill that Democrats and Republicans alike could agree on.

In August 2009 the fight for health care reform lost a great champion. Joe Biden's mentor and longtime friend Ted Kennedy died of brain cancer. Speaking at the memorial service at the Kennedy Library in Boston, Biden told how Kennedy had helped him through his first hard year in the Senate after Neilia's death, and how Kennedy had visited him in Wilmington in 1988 when Biden was recovering from brain surgery. Throughout Kennedy's Senate career, he had fought for universal health care in the United States.

By 2010, Republican resistance to Barack Obama's presidency had grown. But through compromises and pushing and pulling, Congress managed to pass the Patient Protection and Affordable Care Act (ACA, or "Obamacare"). Joe Biden could feel rightly proud of his part in the effort. This was the first major health care reform since the beginning of Medicare in 1966.

On March 23, 2010, Joe Biden went with Barack Obama to the East Room of the White House, where President Obama would finally sign the ACA into law. Biden was so excited that he forgot he was standing next to a live microphone. "Mr. President," he said to Obama, "this is a big [expletive] deal."

One more of Joe Biden's gaffes. But in this case, perhaps, a forgivable one.

Appointing new justices to the Supreme Court was also an important concern of the Obama administration.

In May 2009, President Obama nominated Sonia Sotomayor to replace retiring justice David Souter. Vice President Biden, with his long experience on the Senate Judiciary Committee, was glad to help her get ready for the hearings. Sotomayor sailed through the process and was easily confirmed by the Senate. She was the first Hispanic Supreme Court justice.

A year later, in May 2010, Obama nominated Elena Kagan to replace Justice John Paul Stevens. She, too, was confirmed by the Senate.

Also in May, Joe Biden took a trip that had a bittersweet personal meaning. After giving a commencement speech at Syracuse University, he visited Bellevue Elementary School. There he told the kids about Neilia, "the most beautiful teacher," and how he used to play basketball with her students on the playground as he waited for her.

Along with the Obama administration's victories, they suffered some serious defeats. In the congressional elections of November 2010, Democrats lost control of the House of Representatives by a landslide. "A shellacking," President Obama called it. Now the Democrats would have a harder time passing legislation.

Just as Jill had predicted, living in the vice president's residence in Washington had great advantages. Joe and Jill Biden were delighted to have Hunter and Kathleen and their three children not far away. Hunter had given up his lobbying business, to avoid political embarrassment for his father, and now he had a consulting firm.

Hunter's youngest daughter, Maisy, and Sasha Obama were in the same class at Sidwell Friends School. The two were best friends. Kathleen Biden and Michelle Obama also became close, and the two women and their girls even took vacations together.

As for Beau, he and Hallie stayed in Wilmington. Having returned from his tour in Iraq with his National Guard unit, Beau was now back to working as attorney general of Delaware. And he seemed perfectly fit and healthy, as he always had been.

So it was a shock to the Biden family when suddenly, one day in 2010, Beau woke up paralyzed on his right side. Joe rushed to the hospital, but by then Beau's symptoms had just as quickly disappeared. The doctors decided it wasn't anything serious.

Still, Joe was deeply shaken. And Barack Obama was also worried, because during the previous two years of working together, he and Joe had become friends. When Biden returned to the White House, Obama's senior advisor David Axelrod was startled to see the president *running* down the hall. Barack was running to greet his friend Joe, to give him a big hug.

In 2012, President Obama and Vice President Biden were up for reelection. Their Republican opponents were Mitt Romney, former governor of Massachusetts, and Representative Paul Ryan of Wisconsin. That May, Biden made a campaign appearance on *Meet the Press*. An issue in the news at the time was same-sex marriage, and Obama was still officially against legalizing it.

But Joe Biden, when asked about same-sex marriage by the interviewer, blurted out that he was "absolutely comfortable" with it. Although Biden's previous position was that marriage could be only between a man and a woman, he now believed that marriage was all about the question, "Who do you love?" He believed that gay and lesbian couples were entitled to the same civil rights as straight couples.

President Obama had cautiously, privately come around to this position. But the Obama administration (including Biden) had intended to wait until November, after Obama had been reelected, to publicly announce the change. So Obama was taken aback that Biden had jumped the gun on national television. However, the president set the confusion to rest by announcing his new position on ABC's *Good Morning America*: "I think same-sex couples should be able to get married."

And on Tuesday, November 6, President Barack Obama and Vice President Biden were reelected.

# Chapter 13

# "My Beautiful Boy"

Now President Obama and Vice President Biden had another four years to accomplish their goals for the country. But there was a shadow waiting to fall over Joe's personal life.

In 2012, as Joe won reelection as vice president, Beau Biden easily won reelection as attorney general of Delaware. Joe had great hopes for his older son. He hoped that Beau would follow him into the Senate seat he'd left. And he hoped even more that Beau would run for the presidency one day. Maybe Joe himself could never be president, but he felt sure that Beau could.

Ever since Beau's paralysis scare in 2010, he'd felt fine. Then, in 2013, he began to have symptoms that did not go away. He had dizzy spells; he had hallucinations. That summer, a brain scan showed a large tumor on the left side of his brain. Surgery to remove most of it revealed that it was an aggressive, malignant brain cancer.

Beau's cancer was probably incurable. But he believed in the Biden motto, "If you get knocked down, get up." He was determined to fight his cancer, and he began the attack with radiation and chemotherapy.

"Don't let anybody tell me what the percentages are," Beau told his father and brother. "I'm going to beat this." Throughout his treatment, he continued working as attorney general.

At one point in 2014, Beau was so weakened by his harsh treatment that he thought he might have to resign from his job. Joe worried that Beau and his family would lose their only income, and he and Jill considered taking out a second mortgage on their house. When Barack Obama heard about this, he ordered Joe, "Don't do that." Barack had enough money, and he would lend it to Joe if the Biden family needed it.

But Beau rallied, and in November 2014, he announced his plan to run for governor of Delaware in 2016. For Thanksgiving 2014, the whole Biden family gathered as usual on Nantucket Island. This joyful tradition had started in 1975 with just Joe, Jill, Beau, and Hunter.

As the Bidens had celebrated the holiday together year after year, the family had grown to include Ashley, then the boys' wives, the five grandchildren, and finally Ashley's husband, Howard Krein. For many years, they drove to the Nantucket ferry in a car caravan. But these days, they all flew to the island on Air Force Two, the plane that transports the vice president of the US.

The 2014 Thanksgiving gathering was different. Beau refused to talk about his illness, and he never complained. "All good," he was in the habit of saying. "All good." Beau didn't want anyone to give in to unhappy feelings around him. "Dad!" he reminded Joe, who was gazing at him sadly. "Don't look at me like that."

But Joe and the rest of the Bidens couldn't help worrying. Beau was thin and walking awkwardly, and he got tired quickly. The radiation and chemotherapy had weakened his right arm and leg, and now he had trouble remembering the names of things. Instead of saying, "Pass the dinner rolls," he'd say, "Pass the, you know, the brown thing you put the butter on."

Joe had originally planned to run for president in 2016. If so, he needed to ramp up his campaign in 2015—the earlier, the better. But now he thought he should wait and see how Beau's treatment went.

However, in a private talk during the Thanksgiving vacation, Beau and Hunter disagreed with Joe. They believed that their father was by far the best candidate. "You've got to run. I want you to run," Beau said.

Beau continued to work as Delaware's attorney general through the end of his term, January 2015. In February, the doctors discovered that in spite of chemotherapy and radiation, the tumor in his brain was growing and spreading. Beau decided to keep on fighting with more surgery and an experimental treatment.

The Biden family would do anything for Beau, and they all worked together to support him. Hallie, his wife, made sure that their children, Natalie and Hunter, were well and safe. Jill, his mom, looked out for the smallest details of Beau's comfort.

Hunter, his brother and closest friend, was the person Beau could confide in as he confronted the painful questions of life and death. Ashley, Beau's adoring sister, met him at the hospital in Philadelphia and stayed with him through his therapy sessions. Ashley's husband, Howard, was a head and neck surgeon himself. He was in constant touch with Beau's doctors, and he kept his professional eye on Beau. He was also able to interpret the doctors' medical jargon for the family.

Joe Biden wanted nothing more than to be with his son as Beau fought for his life. But he was the vice president of the United States, with heavy responsibilities. President Obama was counting on him. And most important, Joe knew that Beau himself would be deeply disappointed in his father if he slacked off on his duty to his country.

So Joe continued to work, including overseas travel, sometimes with a grandchild or two. One of the privileges of being vice president was that Biden could take his grandchildren all over the world. Hunter's daughter Finnegan, now sixteen, was especially eager for international adventures, and she was "Pop's" companion for a trip to Europe early in February 2015.

Biden's main reason for this trip was a conference in Munich, Germany. The US and its western European allies were worried about Russia's continuing attacks on Ukraine, in spite of the cease-fire agreement signed in September 2014. In his speech to the conference, Biden told the assembled dignitaries that the US would support Ukraine with military aid if necessary. Senator John McCain, who was head of the US congressional delegation at the conference, told Biden afterward that it was the best speech he'd heard Joe give.

At the beginning of March, it was discovered that Beau's experimental treatment for cancer had failed. Beau took this in calmly, then decided to try more surgery and a combination of two other treatments. One was so new that it had never before been used on humans.

Joe kept on working, so hard that he developed pneumonia himself. But he continued to work. He flew with Jill to Guatemala for a conference with the leaders of that country, El Salvador, and Honduras. Because of the poverty and violence in those countries, a surge of refugees, especially children, were arriving in the US. Biden and the Central American leaders agreed on a plan that provided hope for stabilizing their countries.

Upon Biden's return to the US, the new Iraqi prime minister called on him for help in resisting an invasion. Biden had made many trips to Iraq over the years, first as senator and then as vice president, since President Bush had launched the Iraq War in 2003. And because Beau had risked his life serving in Iraq with the National Guard, Biden felt a personal concern for that country.

Toward the end of March, Biden flew to Houston, where Beau would undergo his next surgery. Joe could see that the doctors and nurses had a special concern for his son. And Beau was truly and lovingly supported by his family, especially Jill; and his wife, Hallie; and Hunter. Ashley was there with her big brother too.

Joe stayed in Houston for two days after the surgery. Visiting the hospital once more before he left, he found Beau up and walking. "It's all good, Dad," said Beau. But Joe hated to leave him. During the flight back to Washington, he wrote in his diary: *I feel so goddam lonely.*

The new experimental treatment seemed to help Beau, and in April he was able to go home to Wilmington. One day he and Hallie brought their children to Joe and Jill's for a special event. Jill had written a children's book, *Don't Forget, God Bless Our Troops*, especially for the children of parents serving in the military overseas. A reading of the book was being recorded for *Reading Rainbow*. Ten-year-old Natalie, eight-year-old Hunter, Jill, and Joe took turns reading aloud for the visiting TV crew.

At times during the reading Joe struggled not to break down, but he felt he had to keep strong for the rest of his family, as well as for Beau and for the country. Back in Washington, Natalie's class went to the capital to tour the White House. Joe and Jill hosted her class for pizza at the vice president's residence.

In May, there seemed to be hope that the latest cancer treatment could work. Beau moved to the Walter Reed National Military Medical Center near Washington, where Joe could visit him twice a day. One evening, Joe arrived at the hospital eager to tell Beau about a visitor to the White House: the singer-songwriter Elton John.

Joe reminded Beau that the two of them and Hunter used to sing along with Elton John on the car radio. There in the hospital room, he sang to Beau: "'But the biggest kick I ever got / Was doing a thing called the Crocodile Rock.'" Beau's eyes were closed, but he smiled.

During the next few weeks, Joe Biden clung to the hope that Beau could survive his illness and the harsh treatments. Sometimes Beau seemed a little better, sometimes worse. Vice President Biden continued to work.

The crisis in Ukraine was mounting. The country had been plagued by corruption for years, and Joe Biden had tried to encourage the government to control it. Now Russian troops were still on the eastern border with heavy artillery. Three months earlier, Russian president Vladimir Putin had signed an agreement to withdraw his troops, but he still hadn't done it. Worse, he seemed to be preparing for a fresh push into Ukraine.

On Friday, May 30, Joe and the rest of the Bidens gathered at the hospital for a conference with the doctors. The doctors presented the medical details but didn't say what they added up to. Finally Howard, the only doctor in the Biden family, said, "You have to tell them the truth." The truth was, there was no more hope.

At a little before eight o'clock that evening, Beau's heart stopped beating. Later that night, Joe wrote in his diary: *It happened. My God, my boy. My beautiful boy.*

Beau's memorial service was held on Saturday, June 6, 2015, at St. Anthony of Padua Church in

Wilmington. It was a public event, recorded by TV cameras, since Beau as well as his father had been a public figure. Hunter and Ashley both spoke touchingly about their brother, and President Obama gave the main eulogy. Barack Obama did not often let his emotions show, but this day he spoke from the heart. He praised Beau. He told Joe with tears in his eyes how much Joe's friendship meant to him.

Obama ended by saying that he and Michelle and their girls considered themselves honorary members of the Biden family. "We're always here for you," he promised. "We always will be. My word as a Biden." As Barack left the podium, he and Joe embraced each other.

Joe Biden was still considering a run for president in 2016. In January 2017 he would be seventy-four, older than any other president-elect in the history of the US, so maybe this was his last chance. Beau had believed in him so deeply; Beau had declared that it was his father's *duty* to run. "You've got to run. I want you to run."

However, President Obama advised Biden against running. Obama thought that Joe and his family had been through too much, with Beau's illness and death, to take on the huge stress of a presidential campaign. He also thought that Hillary Clinton had a better chance of beating the Republican candidate, whoever that turned out to be.

In spite of Obama's advice, in September 2015, Biden's team convinced him that he did have a decent chance. Joe began appearing and giving speeches, and he felt good about it. He was fired up, jogging through applauding crowds and speaking expressively on *The Late Show with Stephen Colbert*.

Then the political attacks began, and Biden realized how nasty the campaign was going to get. There were rumors that Joe was using sympathy for Beau's death to boost his run for president. Late in October, he painfully decided to end his campaign. He made the announcement the next day in the White House Rose Garden, with Jill on one side and Barack Obama on the other.

Vice President Joe Biden kept on working. He knew it was his duty, and he knew it was what Beau would have wanted him to do. In December 2015 he flew to Ukraine to speak to the Ukrainian parliament. This country was a struggling democracy, threatened by Russia and by its own corruption in the government.

Meanwhile, seventeen Republicans competed to be nominated as the party's presidential candidate. At first, one of the least likely candidates seemed to be Donald J. Trump. Trump was a TV reality show star and real-estate magnate, and he had no previous experience in the military or in politics. Nevertheless, he won the primary elections in state after state. By the end of May, Trump was guaranteed the Republican nomination.

Hillary Clinton won the Democratic nomination, seriously challenged only by Senator Bernie Sanders of Vermont. During the summer and fall of 2016, public opinion polls seemed to show that she would win the general election. And Trump continued to behave in ways that would seem to doom his election chances.

Donald Trump made openly racist remarks. During a rally in Iowa, he belittled Senator John McCain, a decorated war hero. Later, Trump disrespected the father of a soldier who had died in combat. A video was discovered in which he'd bragged about sexually assaulting women, and it went viral. Some political observers thought that the Republican Party, represented by a candidate as unqualified for the presidency and as divisive as Trump, was doomed.

And yet Donald Trump's message had a strong

appeal, especially to white working-class voters. They felt disrespected by politicians like Barack Obama and Hillary Clinton, the "liberal elite." They felt uneasy about the way American culture was changing, and Trump's slogan, "Make America Great Again," promised to restore the good old days.

Most important, Trump promised to bring back the decent jobs that these workers used to count on, such as in manufacturing and coal mining. He promised a trillion-dollar infrastructure program to provide hundreds of thousands of new construction jobs. He promised to protect US borders from Latin American immigrants. In fact, he promised to find and remove all undocumented immigrants from the US.

On election night, November 8, even as Hillary Clinton's followers gathered for a huge victory party, the returns came in for Donald Trump. Very early on November 9, the TV networks declared Trump the winner. The final electoral vote was Trump 306, Clinton 232. Donald Trump would become the forty-fifth president of the United States.

## The Electoral College

In the United States, the president is not elected by the *popular* vote, the total of all votes cast throughout the country. Instead the president is actually elected by the Electoral College, established in 1789 by the Constitution. The Constitution provides that each state has a certain number of electoral votes, which equals that state's number of representatives (different for each state) plus the number of senators (always two).

The results of the popular vote and the electoral vote are usually the same, but not always. Five times in the history of the US, the winner of the popular vote for president has lost the election. In the election of 2000, the decision between George W. Bush and Al Gore came down to the twenty-five electoral votes of one state, Florida. And the popular vote in Florida was so close that the Supreme Court finally decided the election.

Election 2016 was a hard year for Joe Biden. It was the first year after Beau's death. Joe didn't have the exciting challenge of running for president. And the Obama administration struggled to accomplish their goals. Since the 2014 congressional elections, the Republicans had had majorities in both the House of Representatives and the Senate, and they were determined to block Obama at every turn.

In March 2016, Obama had nominated Judge Merrick Garland to fill a vacancy on the Supreme Court. Judge Garland was considered highly qualified, and he was politically moderate, which Obama thought would make him acceptable to the conservatives. But the Republican Senate refused to consider the nomination, claiming that a president should not appoint a new justice during his last year in office.

And when Hillary Clinton lost the election in November, it was the crowning blow to Obama and Biden. If Clinton had been the next president, they could have been sure that she would carry forward their work. With Donald Trump in the White House, they could be sure he would not.

One of Barack Obama's last acts as president was to throw a surprise party for Joe Biden. It was January 12, 2017, eight days before Donald Trump's inauguration. Biden was told that he and Jill were invited to meet Barack and Michelle for a quiet toast to their eight-year partnership. But when Joe saw the spacious White House State Dining Room filled with guests and TV cameras, he knew something was up.

However, even when Obama called him up to the podium, even when he named Joe Biden "the best vice president America's ever had," Biden still didn't know what Obama was going to do. After an affectionate, teasing speech full of praise for Joe as a friend and a public servant, Barack sprung the real surprise. He was awarding Joseph Robinette Biden Jr. the Presidential Medal of Freedom.

As Obama hung the medal around his neck, Joe looked stunned. He knew he was supposed to say something, but for once he was speechless. It took him several minutes to pull himself together. Finally he answered the president's tribute with a heartfelt reply.

In the long history of US presidents and their vice presidents, there had never been a pair like Barack and Joe. They were not just two politicians yoked together to balance the Democratic or Republican ticket. They were working partners—but not only partners, either. They were close and loving friends.

# Chapter 14

# "Promise Me, Dad"

Was Joe Biden's political career at an end? In January 2017, as Joe and Jill left the vice president's residence, many people assumed so. After all, the next election was in 2020, the year that Biden would turn seventy-eight. If elected, he would be the oldest president in US history by several years.

But he still wanted the job. Biden thought—and even said publicly—that he believed he could have won the 2016 election: "I thought I was a great candidate." He said frankly that he never thought Hillary Clinton was a great candidate, although he thought she would have been a good president.

In November 2017, Joe Biden published a new book, *Promise Me, Dad*, about Beau's illness and death. "Promise me, Dad," was what Beau had demanded of his father. Beau wanted to know that whatever happened to him, his father would be "all right." And Joe had promised, giving "my word as a Biden."

What did "all right" mean? Joe believed it meant that he could not give up on life. And the two most important things in his life had always been his family and his work. His life's work, in government, might not be over. He could run for president one more time, in 2020.

During the next four years, the Trump administration set about to roll back all the achievements of the eight Obama-Biden years. He immediately announced his intention to destroy the Affordable Care Act (Obamacare). He called the danger of global climate change a "hoax," and he threatened to pull the US out of the Paris Agreement, in which the nations of the world had agreed to reduce their greenhouse gases. President Trump seemed determined to push away America's closest allies. He talked of leaving the North Atlantic Treaty Organization (NATO), a key alliance between the US and western Europe since 1949.

With the help of the Republican-majority Congress, President Trump passed legislation giving large tax breaks to the wealthy. He appointed two conservative judges to the Supreme Court. He replaced federal officials with ones who would favor private schools over public schools, or remove regulations on water pollution. He encouraged harsh treatment, such as separating children from their parents, of immigrants from Latin America.

Russia, it turned out, had tried to interfere in the 2016 US election. This was the conclusion of the FBI and the CIA, but Trump pooh-poohed it. At a summit meeting with the Russian president, Vladimir Putin, Trump asked if they had tried to interfere. Putin said no, and Trump seemed to take his word for it. President Trump acted friendly, even admiringly, toward Putin. He also praised the brutal dictators Kim Jong-un of North Korea and Rodrigo Duterte of the Philippines.

In 2017 the Republicans had majorities in the House of Representatives and the Senate, and this seemed like their chance to accomplish all their conservative goals at once. Soon after Trump's inauguration, the Republicans in Congress launched a bill meant to kill the Affordable Care Act. They called the legislation "Repeal and Replace," but in fact it would take medical insurance away from many millions of

Americans. When a pared-down version of "Repeal and Replace" came up for approval in the Senate in July, it seemed sure to pass. Biden's Republican friend Senator John McCain didn't like the bill, but he was home in Arizona, undergoing surgery.

But McCain, like the Bidens, was a tough man to keep down. After the surgery, he flew to Washington and walked onto the Senate floor with stitches over his right eye—and voted thumbs-down on "Repeal and Replace" to break a tie vote. Biden must have appreciated his friend's dramatic moment in the political spotlight, but he also felt the pain of his bad news. John McCain, like Joe's son Beau, had an especially malignant form of brain cancer, and he would die the next year.

In the congressional elections of 2018, a strong reaction against President Trump's policies helped Democrats, especially women, take back the House of Representatives. But Senator Mitch McConnell, who had worked tirelessly for the previous ten years against the goals of Obama's administration, was still majority leader of the Senate. When the House sent bills to the Senate for approval, McConnell refused to even let them come up for debate. Because he killed so many bills this way, he got the nickname "the Grim Reaper."

On April 25, 2019, Joe Biden announced that he was running for president in 2020. He was joining an already crowded Democratic field: Senator Elizabeth Warren of Massachusetts, Senator Amy Klobuchar of Minnesota, Senator Kamala Harris of California, to name only a few. Senator Bernie Sanders of Vermont was also running again. In total, twenty-nine Democratic candidates would declare.

As soon as Biden declared, questions arose about whether he was physically fit, at his age, to run for president. He got a dubious endorsement from Dr. Neal Kassell, the brain surgeon who had operated on Biden's aneurysms in 1988. He joked, "Joe Biden of all of the politicians in Washington is the only one that I'm certain has a brain, because I have seen it. That's more than I can say about all the other candidates or the incumbents."

The Democratic debates began on June 26, 2019, when the polls showed Joe Biden as the Democratic front-runner. In that debate, Senator Kamala Harris of California made news for her dramatic attack on Biden. "I do not believe you are a racist," she began. But she went on to reproach him for voting in the Senate in the 1970s against public-school busing. "There was a little girl in California who was part of the second class to integrate her public schools, and she was bused to school every day. And that little girl was me."

Biden looked shocked, and when he answered Harris, he seemed defensive and off-balance. Jill was shocked too. It "felt like a punch in the gut," she said later.

Over the course of the following debates, other candidates accused Biden of clinging to Obamacare, a flawed health care program; of being beholden to the credit card industries in Delaware for donations; of voting for the Iraq War in 2002; and in general of not being the "new blood" that the Democratic Party needed.

They pointed out the harm done by the 1984 Comprehensive Crime Control Act and the crime reform laws of 1994. And Biden had to admit that the harsh drug laws, resulting in huge prison populations, had been a mistake. The critics brought up many of Biden's numerous slips of the tongue, including the time he called Obama "clean" and "articulate."

In spite of all these attacks, Biden remained the Democratic front-runner through the rest of 2019. And Donald Trump must have believed that Joe

Biden was his most dangerous rival, because he tried to slander Biden as corrupt, as using his political power to benefit himself. During the summer of 2019, Trump pressured the new president of Ukraine, Volodymyr Zelensky, to investigate Joe and his son Hunter for supposed wrongdoing in that country.

It was true that Hunter Biden had served on the board of directors of Burisma, a Ukrainian energy company, from 2014 to April 2019. It was true that Burisma had paid Hunter as much as $50,000 a month. But it was not true that Joe Biden had used his influence in Ukraine to protect his son from investigation.

Trump's effort to pressure a foreign government to harm a political rival became public in September 2019. The Democratic-majority House of Representatives began an investigation that led to President Trump's impeachment on December 18. The House accused him of "abuse of power"—asking a foreign government to help his reelection—and "obstruction of Congress"—refusing to let White House officials testify or turn over documents. The case then moved to the Senate for trial, and without calling witnesses, the Republican-majority Senate voted on February 5, 2020, to acquit the president on both charges.

# Impeachment

The Constitution states that the House of Representatives may *impeach* a president—bring charges against him—for "treason, bribery, or other high crimes and misdemeanors." If they do, the charges are sent to the Senate, which then holds a trial of the accused president. If the Senate votes—by a two-thirds supermajority—to convict, the president will be removed from office. This has never actually happened.

The president has been impeached only three times in US history. In 1868, Andrew Johnson was impeached by the House of Representatives but acquitted by the Senate. Bill Clinton was likewise impeached but acquitted in 1999. In 1974, Richard Nixon was threatened with impeachment, but he resigned before charges could be brought against him.

The trouble with the phrase "high crimes and misdemeanors" is that it's not very precise. It can be interpreted in different ways, so there is a temptation to interpret it against a political opponent, or for a political ally. But Donald Trump's was the first totally partisan impeachment. No Republicans in the House voted to

impeach on either of the two charges, "abuse
of power" or "obstruction of Congress." And in
the Senate trial, every Republican except one
voted to acquit on both charges.

Since Congress was so clearly divided along party
lines, the impeachment process worsened the divisions
in the country. It seemed possible that Donald Trump,
in spite of the extreme dislike many Americans felt for
him, would be reelected in November. His strongest
point was the thriving US economy, although income
inequality had increased.

Meanwhile, the Democratic primary elections
began early in February 2020. Suddenly Joe Biden
was running way behind, coming in fourth in the
Iowa caucuses and then fifth in the New Hampshire
election. The front-runner was now Senator Bernie
Sanders of Vermont. Sanders was a year older than
Biden, but many Democrats felt he was the best
candidate to fight against racial injustice and economic
inequality.

Back in the spring of 2019, a new criticism of
Joe Biden had been brought up as part of the Me
Too movement. The intention of this movement was
to make visible and to stop the sexual harassment

and assault of women by powerful men. Joe Biden's style of interacting with everyone—not just women—had always been physically affectionate. His natural instinct was to like everyone, and to demonstrate how much he liked them by touching, hugging, and giving shoulder rubs.

Many people liked him for it, while others thought it was just Joe being Joe. But a number of women spoke up about feeling that Biden had invaded their personal space. In response, Biden apologized publicly for the times he'd made women uncomfortable.

In March 2020 the issue came up again. A woman who had worked for a short time in Senator Biden's office accused him of sexually assaulting her in 1993. But other people who worked for Joe Biden during that time found the charge frankly unbelievable. And Biden denied it absolutely. After investigating the story, the major news media concluded there was little substance to it.

In the important South Carolina primary at the end of February, Biden's lagging campaign got a big boost. He was endorsed by the influential congressman Jim Clyburn, and he won every county in the state. And on so-called Super Tuesday, March 3, when 1,344 electoral votes were at stake, Biden again won big. He went on to win eighteen of the next twenty-six Democratic primaries.

On April 8, Biden's last rival, Bernie Sanders, dropped out of the race and endorsed Biden for president. On June 6, it became official: Joe Biden, with more than 1,991 delegates, was the presumptive Democratic nominee.

But back in March, the United States had been engulfed by a threat that drew Americans' attention from the presidential race. A new virus, causing a disease called COVID-19, had arisen in China and quickly spread around the globe. It was a coronavirus, like the viruses that cause the common cold, but more infectious and much more deadly. There was no vaccine—and no cure.

## Pandemics

An epidemic is an outbreak of disease that rapidly infects a large number of people in one country or region. A pandemic is an epidemic that spreads quickly through many countries and continents, even worldwide. One of the worst was the Spanish flu of 1918–19, an influenza pandemic that started toward the end of World War I. That highly contagious and often deadly disease infected one-third of the world's population. In the United States, 675,000 people died.

Some serious infectious diseases, such as polio, have been controlled by vaccines, which protect people against infection. Other viruses can be treated with prescription medications to lessen the effects of the disease. But even without a vaccine or treatment, a pandemic can be controlled by preventing the disease's spread in a combination of ways.

Keeping infected people away from healthy people is one important action. Hygiene, such as washing hands and sanitizing surfaces; social distancing, such as avoiding crowds or any close contact; and wearing face masks, to keep infectious droplets out of the air, are all ways to reduce the spread of some viruses.

Epidemiologists—public health professionals who study outbreaks of infectious diseases—warned that the government needed to act immediately, or COVID-19 could kill millions of Americans. Back in 2014, when the dangerous Ebola virus had arrived in the US, the Obama administration had successfully controlled the outbreak. But by 2020, the US was not prepared to fight an invading virus.

At first President Trump was distracted from this danger by his impeachment and by the following trial in the Senate, which ended only at the beginning of February. On February 29, the state of Washington reported the first US death from COVID-19. Trump dismissed the danger of the pandemic. He did bar travelers from China, but by that time, the virus was already established in the US and spreading by leaps and bounds.

By the end of March, the US had 160,000 reported cases of COVID-19, more than any other country in the world. The US death toll from the virus passed 3,000. Since the virus was usually spread by droplets in the air, experts said the best way to keep the pandemic from getting worse was to stop people from breathing, coughing, or sneezing in one another's faces.

Health officials recommended that people stay home and away from others as much as possible, and to wear face masks when they had to go out. In some states and cities, governors and mayors ordered social distancing and even lockdown measures. Businesses, except for necessary ones like hospitals or trash pickup, were ordered to close.

These actions saved lives, but as a result of the lockdown, the national economy slumped. Many businesses failed. Week after week, millions of unemployed workers applied for state aid. By April the unemployment rate rose to almost 15 percent, the worst since the Great Depression of the 1930s.

People who couldn't pay their rent were being evicted from their homes, and millions more lived on the edge of becoming homeless. And many, including children, were going hungry. Lines at food banks stretched for miles. In Congress, Democrats and Republicans worked together to respond to the emergency, passing the Coronavirus Aid, Relief, and Economic Security (CARES) Act, and it was signed into law by President Trump on March 27. The $2.2 trillion was the largest economic stimulus bill ever passed by Congress. The CARES Act provided direct payments by check and unemployment insurance supplements to individual Americans, aid to local and state governments, and loans to businesses.

In spite of efforts to enforce social distancing and lockdowns, the number of deaths in the US from COVID-19 continued to soar, from around one hundred in mid-March to over 103,000 at the end of May. But President Trump still refused to admit how serious the pandemic was.

For some weeks the president held daily press conferences on the coronavirus, but he often contradicted his own medical experts or turned from discussing the pandemic to criticizing his opponents. He resisted mobilizing the nation in order to supply hospitals with masks and other protective equipment, or to make testing for the virus widely available. He insisted that individual states and cities were responsible for combatting the virus. He would not even set an example for the nation by wearing a mask himself.

From March to May, many Democrats complained about "Biden in the Basement," Joe Biden's low-key presidential campaign. Because of the lockdown, he didn't travel. He set up a studio in his basement and gave interviews and "town meetings" from there, but it wasn't satisfactory campaigning. Biden was at his best with a live audience, mixing with the crowd, looking into people's eyes, shaking hands, hugging.

Then still another national crisis pushed even the pandemic from the headlines. On May 25, four police officers in Minneapolis, Minnesota, arrested George Floyd, a Black man, on suspicion of a nonviolent crime. The officers handcuffed Floyd and, as Floyd lay facedown, one white officer knelt on his neck for more than eight minutes, causing his death. This incident, captured on video, went viral on the Internet. Several similar incidents had been shown on video in recent years, but this was the most shocking, and perhaps the last straw.

A movement with the slogan "Black Lives Matter" had already been active for several years, but now a wave of protest demonstrations swept over the country. The marchers, many white people as well as people of color, chanted George Floyd's last words, "I can't breathe." Joe and Jill Biden visited Floyd's family in Houston to offer their sympathy.

President Trump's reaction was to urge governors to "dominate" the protesters. On the night of June 1, Trump had troops forcefully clear demonstrators out of the park across from the White House. He then walked through the park to a church and posed for a photograph, holding a Bible. Seemingly this act was meant as a signal to conservative Christians that he was on the side of God.

Many political commentators continued to wonder

why Joe Biden wasn't campaigning more aggressively. Even with the pandemic's restrictions on travel and political rallies, they thought he could do more to capture the public's attention. But others pointed out that President Trump, with all his tweeting and press conferences and Rose Garden announcements, was steadily turning voters against himself. There was a saying in politics: "When your opponent is busy digging his own grave, don't take the shovel away from him."

On June 2, Joe Biden traveled to Philadelphia to give a speech to the nation. Standing against a background of American flags, he spoke to the protesters about the kind of president he would be. "I'll seek to heal the racial wounds that have long plagued our country, not use them for political gain." And he asked the nation, "Look at where we are now and think anew: Is this who we are? Is this who we want to be?"

By mid-June, 115,000 Americans had died from the coronavirus. The president's approval rating sank to 38 percent. Six weeks later, over 150,000 Americans had died, and the virus was spreading uncontrolled. The Black Lives Matter demonstrations continued in cities around the country, including Seattle, Chicago, and New York.

President Trump seemed desperate to reopen and revive the national economy, which had been his biggest political advantage. Also, he was distressed at not being able to speak in front of applauding crowds. In June, against public health advice, he held his first rally in months at an indoor arena in Tulsa, Oklahoma. Not as many people as expected showed up, perhaps put off by the health risk.

In the history of the United States, there had never been a presidential election year like this, without numerous rallies and noisy, crowded conventions. The Democratic National Party announced in July that their convention would take place online. The Republican National Party moved its convention plans from Charlotte, North Carolina, to Jacksonville, Florida, trying to avoid coronavirus restrictions. But by late July they had shrunk their convention plans to a one-day business meeting only, back in Charlotte. However, in a few weeks these plans would change again, dramatically.

President Trump could no longer claim a healthy economy; few Americans even believed the economy could recover before the next year. National polls showed Joe Biden with a significant lead over Donald Trump. The Trump campaign searched for the best way to turn voters against Biden.

One tack was to portray the former vice president as too old for the job of president. But Donald Trump was only four years younger than Joe Biden, and clearly overweight in contrast to trim, fit Biden. Another approach was to accuse Biden of going senile, based on his public slips of the tongue. But Trump himself made rambling, sometimes incoherent speeches, and he was mocked for boasting of a high score on his ten-minute test for dementia.

Trump repeatedly warned against mail-in voting. He claimed—against the evidence—that mail-in ballots could easily be faked. He suggested that the general election in November might have to be delayed because of the pandemic. However, even Republicans in Congress quickly pointed out that only Congress had the power to change an election date.

As the Black Lives Matter protests continued, Trump portrayed himself as the "law and order" president. He sent federal troops to Portland, Oregon, and other cities to quash the demonstrations. His campaign made a special appeal to women in the suburbs, where he had done well in 2016. But polls showed that suburban voters actually supported the protests, and they disapproved of Trump's handling of the crisis.

Still, Biden's campaign knew better than to count on the polls. After all, in the fall of 2016, Hillary Clinton had led Donald Trump in the polls, right up until the November election.

Biden still had to pick a vice presidential running mate. He promised to choose a woman, and he promised to announce his choice before the Democratic National Convention in late August.

# Chapter 15

# President Joe Biden

On Tuesday, August 17, Joe Biden made a video-conference call. He asked the woman on the screen, "You ready to go to work?"

"Oh my God, I am so ready," answered Kamala Harris. The senator from California, daughter of immigrants from India and Jamaica, was Biden's choice for his vice presidential running mate.

Joe Biden sent out an email to his supporters, explaining why he'd chosen Senator Harris. "Smart, tough, and ready to lead," he said of her. As he'd promised several months before, he'd picked a woman. Many of his advisors had thought he should pick a woman of color, and Kamala Harris was mixed-race Black and Indian.

Also important, Joe Biden wanted a running

mate whom he felt comfortable with. Kamala Harris's political positions, like Biden's, were liberal, but not far left. And Biden already knew Harris through his son Beau. When Beau Biden had been attorney general of Delaware, she'd been attorney general of California. The two AGs had been friends, and Beau had respected her work highly.

Some commentators were surprised that Biden would pick someone who'd attacked him so forcefully on the debate stage just a year before. But Joe Biden didn't hold grudges. And he wasn't afraid of strong women.

"Uniting America" was the theme of the Democratic National Convention in 2020. Because of the COVID-19 virus, it was unlike any other convention in the history of the United States. Back in March 2019, the Democratic Convention had been planned to take place in Milwaukee, Wisconsin, in July 2020. But by the summer of 2020 the coronavirus pandemic was raging. It wouldn't have been safe for fifty thousand speakers, delegates, reporters, and volunteers to crowd together.

The dates of the convention were changed to August 17–20. Most of the events of the convention had to be recorded beforehand, or take place elsewhere and be broadcast live. Even Joe Biden and Kamala Harris did not travel to Milwaukee to accept their nominations. And no one spoke to a large live audience, to receive roars of applause.

However, the online format was a chance to include many ordinary people. One of the most touching appearances was by Brayden Harrington, a thirteen-year-old boy who stuttered. He'd met Joe Biden in New Hampshire early in the year, and Biden had taken time to talk with him one-on-one about how to overcome his stutter. "Joe Biden made me more confident about something that's bothered me my whole life," said Harrington. "Joe Biden cared. Imagine what he could do for all of us."

Naturally, many well-known Democrats, including both Michelle and Barack Obama, praised Biden during the convention. But there were also a surprising number of high-profile Republicans speaking up for Joe. One of these was Cindy McCain, wife of the late senator John McCain of Arizona. She described Biden as a politician who fought hard for what he believed—but got things done in the government by reaching out to those who disagreed with him, like McCain.

The following Monday, August 24, the Republican

National Convention opened in Charlotte, North Carolina. Because of the pandemic, many of these speakers were also recorded without an audience. But on August 27, President Trump gave his acceptance speech on the South Lawn of the White House, in front of a close-packed audience of over a thousand, most without face masks. Aside from the danger of spreading the virus, many were shocked that a president running for reelection would use the White House as a backdrop for a campaign speech. Federal law forbids the use of federal property for political campaigns, although technically the president is exempt from this law.

A major theme of the Republican Convention was that Joe Biden as president would be the front for the "radical left." A TV ad for Trump had warned, "You won't be safe in Joe Biden's America." Speakers accused Biden of being a socialist and of wanting to protect criminals from law-abiding citizens, instead of the other way around. President Trump predicted that if Biden won, the country would be taken over by "violent anarchists" who would destroy America.

In response, Joe Biden pointed out that the riots and shootings were taking place during *Donald Trump's* presidency. And Trump himself was inciting violence, "pouring gasoline on the fire." As for Biden, he said, "I condemn violence of every kind by anyone, whether on the left or the right."

Political commentators noted that in 1968, Richard Nixon had won the presidency by promising, as Trump was doing now, to restore "law and order." But one important difference was that Nixon had not yet been president, so he could logically blame the turmoil of 1968 on eight years of Democratic rule. Not so for Donald Trump, Joe Biden reminded voters in a speech in Pittsburgh on August 31. "He keeps telling us if he was president you'd feel safe," Biden remarked dryly. "Well, he is president, whether he knows it or not."

During the conventions and for weeks afterward, Black Lives Matter protest marches continued. The vast majority of these protests were peaceful, but the media emphasized any incidents of vandalism, looting, or violent clashes with counter-protesters or the police. Americans' support for the demonstrators dropped off. Two protesters were killed in Kenosha, Wisconsin, allegedly by an illegally armed militia member, and a far-right demonstrator was shot and killed in Portland, Oregon. The alleged shooter in Portland was hunted down and killed by federal marshals.

Although the presidential election always gets the most national attention, both the Republican and the Democratic Parties were especially concerned about the Senate races this year. What if Joe Biden won the presidency, but the Republicans kept their majority in the Senate? They could make it very difficult for the Biden administration to achieve its goals, just as they had during President Obama's second term.

On the other hand, what if President Trump was reelected but the Democrats won the majority in the Senate and kept their majority in the House of Representatives? If their majorities were large enough, they would have the chance to enact the laws they favored. Although the president has the power to veto a bill passed by Congress, a two-thirds majority in Congress can override a veto. And a majority-Democratic Congress might even decide to impeach and try President Trump again.

In the last weeks of the presidential race of 2020, Americans grew more and more anxious. They were worried about the nation's racial problems. They were worried about the ongoing pandemic, which had claimed two hundred thousand American lives as of September 22.

Large numbers of Americans were worried about losing their jobs, or even about getting enough help to pay their rent and feed their families. Even before the COVID-19 pandemic, thirty-five million Americans, including ten million children, had not had enough to eat. Now millions more joined the long lines at overwhelmed food banks.

On top of these anxieties, many Americans also worried that the election would not be decided fairly. US intelligence officials announced that Russia was trying to influence American voters, as they had in 2016, this time by spreading misinformation about Biden. Also, more voters than ever planned to mail in their ballots, rather than vote at a polling place, because they were afraid of catching the deadly COVID-19 virus. But Trump's postmaster general was cutting back on mail services and removing mail drop boxes from neighborhoods. And President Trump warned over and over, against all the evidence, that voting by mail was open to fraud.

Joe Biden was prepared to fight back for a fair election. He had assembled a team of hundreds of lawyers to see to it that the election was conducted and decided according to law. They would monitor each state, especially the battleground states, to watch how votes were cast and counted. They would make sure that people knew how to vote, and that all citizens entitled to vote had the chance to do so. They would also be on the watch for foreign interference in the election.

Meanwhile, Democrats were also concerned about a longer-term threat: an inaccurate count of the national census. Every ten years, the US Census Bureau is required by the Constitution to count the total number of people residing in each state. In 2020, because of the COVID-19 pandemic, the Census Bureau had begun door-to-door collection of information later than usual. And now the Trump administration announced it was ending the census a month early.

Each once-in-a-decade census count is important, because the population of each state determines the number of congressmen or congresswomen that state sends to the House of Representatives. The count also determines the number of electors who vote in the Electoral College to choose the president. And the fédéral government uses the census information to decide how much money to send each state for needs such as health clinics, schools, and highways.

But in 2020, because so many Americans had fallen into poverty and even homelessness during the pandemic, it was more difficult for the census to reach them. And for fear of deportation, many families with undocumented immigrants avoided giving the government any information. Democrats accused the Trump administration of deliberately undercounting these people, who tended to vote Democratic.

As the campaign neared its end, Donald Trump threw out one unsupported claim after another. He implied several times that Biden was taking performance-enhancing drugs for his public appearances. On September 16 he announced that his "Operation Warp Speed" project to develop a vaccine for COVID-19 would produce a vaccine and distribute it to all Americans "in a matter of weeks." Medical experts, however, agreed that this schedule was not possible. Even if a safe and effective vaccine were available by the end of 2020, it would take several months to distribute it to the whole population.

Most alarming of all, President Trump seemed to be signaling that he would not accept defeat, even if Biden won the election. At the opening of the Republican Convention, Trump had declared, "The only way they can take this election away from us is if this is a rigged election." At a rally in Nevada on

September 12, Trump opened his speech with, "I am going to start by saying that the Democrats are trying to rig this election because it's the only way they are going to win."

At a news conference on September 23, President Trump refused to commit to a peaceful transfer of power after the November election. He repeated the false claim that mail-in ballots were open to fraud. Meanwhile, the polls continued to show that nationally, Joe Biden was keeping a steady lead over Donald Trump. In several of the battleground states — Michigan, Pennsylvania, and Wisconsin — Biden seemed likely to win. In Florida and Arizona, he was even with Trump.

By the end of September, 90 percent of likely voters had already made up their minds, and some of them had already voted. Although Election Day was officially November 3, it had evolved into "Election Season." Early voting started on September 18 in Minnesota, South Dakota, and Wyoming, and only fifteen of the fifty states had no early voting.

Besides campaigning for reelection, Republicans were striving to achieve one particular goal before the end of President Trump's term. They hoped to place another conservative justice on the Supreme Court, giving the conservatives a firm 6–3 majority. Then they might finally be able to overturn *Roe v. Wade* and the Affordable Care Act (Obamacare). Also, if the presidential election results were extremely close, as they had been in 2000, the Supreme Court might make the final decision about whether Joe Biden or Donald Trump had won.

On September 18, Associate Justice Ruth Bader Ginsberg died at the age of eighty-seven, so now a seat on the court was vacant. The next day, Senate Majority Leader Mitch McConnell announced that the Senate would vote on Trump's nominee for the court before the election. The following week President Trump named his choice, appellate judge Amy Coney Barrett.

Democrats were outraged. McConnell and the Republican senators had claimed it was wrong for President Obama to nominate a Supreme Court justice during 2016, his last year in office. Now these same senators insisted that it was the president's duty to fill a vacancy on the court. But no matter how much the Democrats protested, Trump and the Senate did have the legal right to nominate and confirm a new Supreme Court justice. On October 26, Judge

Barrett was confirmed by the Republican majority in the Senate.

The first presidential debate took place on September 29 at Case Reserve Western University in Cleveland, Ohio, moderated by Chris Wallace of Fox News. Many observers judged it the worst presidential debate ever. For over an hour and a half, Trump interrupted and talked loudly over Biden, in spite of the moderator's reminders that both sides had agreed *not* to interrupt. A few times Biden lost his temper, exclaiming, "Will you shut up, man?" and calling President Trump a "clown."

However, Joe Biden did manage to make a few points between Trump's interruptions. When Trump tried to throw him off-balance by slandering Hunter, Biden turned and spoke directly into the cameras. "This is not about my family or his family," he told the audience watching at home. "It's about your family, the American people. He doesn't want to talk about what you need."

In spite of the disorderly debate, two meaningful facts came out: Trump still refused to agree that he would accept the results of the election, and he repeated false claims that mail-in ballots were often fraudulent. He also refused to condemn violence committed by white supremacist groups, and even seemed to encourage them.

And only a week after the debate, the FBI had shocking news for the country. They had arrested thirteen members of an armed militia group that had been plotting to kidnap the governor of Michigan, Gretchen Whitmer. The domestic terrorists' goal had been to take over the state government and launch a civil war before the election.

In the debate, President Trump had mocked Biden for wearing a mask to protect against COVID-19. Two days later he assured the guests at a charity dinner that "the end of the pandemic is in sight." The next morning, October 2, Trump announced that he and the First Lady had tested positive for the COVID-19 virus. That evening he was admitted to Walter Reed National Military Medical Center.

President Trump was given oxygen at least once and was treated with a combination of medications usually reserved for seriously ill patients. However, he insisted in tweets and on video that he was recovering quickly. In fact, he left the hospital only three days later, posed on the White House balcony removing his mask, and urged the nation not to be afraid of the coronavirus.

People diagnosed with COVID-19 are advised by the Centers for Disease Control and Prevention (CDC) to isolate themselves for at least ten days after the first symptoms. However, on October 10, President Trump declared at a rally at the White House that he was "immune" and not infectious. On October 12 he launched a strenuous week of back-to-back, in-person rallies in Florida, Pennsylvania, Iowa, North Carolina, and Wisconsin, for starters. He intended to hold two or three such events every day until November 3.

In contrast, Joe Biden continued to campaign steadily but safely. In Toledo, Ohio, on October 12, he spoke outside, in a United Auto Workers union hall parking lot, to an audience in American-made cars. Biden reminded them how in 2009, during the Great Recession, he and President Obama had rescued the US auto industry. At the applause lines, the listeners honked their approval.

In spite of Trump's efforts to de-emphasize the COVID-19 pandemic, it was topmost on the minds of most Americans. And most Americans blamed President Trump for mishandling the US response to the disease. It had been revealed recently that Trump had known since January how deadly the coronavirus was, but had deliberately downplayed the danger.

Since March, the lethal virus had disrupted Americans' lives, and it continued to do so. The school year had begun, but a large proportion of schools still could not hold in-person classes, or offered them only half the time, in a "hybrid" schedule. By October 14, more than 216,000 Americans had died of the disease, and more than a million worldwide had lost a father or mother, a brother or sister, a grandparent, a dear friend.

And although, as Trump pointed out, the stock market was doing well, ordinary Americans were struggling to make ends meet. The money from the one-time direct payments to individuals from the CARES Act had run out quickly, and the increased unemployment benefits had ended, or would end soon. A chorus of economists, corporate executives, and business leaders, as well as workers, warned that the US economy faced disaster unless Congress passed a second economic stimulus bill. They urged the president and the Senate to work with the House of Representatives and pass a rescue package before the election.

On October 7, Senator Kamala Harris had met Vice President Mike Pence at the University of Utah in Salt Lake City for the vice presidential debate. She'd called the Trump administration's response to the pandemic "the greatest failure of any presidential administration in the history of our country." She'd also accused Trump and the Republican Senate of ramming through the confirmation of a conservative Supreme Court justice, rather than passing a desperately needed economic stimulus bill for the American people.

Joe Biden's lead over Donald Trump continued to grow slightly, but there was concern that no matter who won, the result might not be clear for several days or even weeks. That would be different from most past presidential elections, when the results had been clear by late on election night, or early the next morning. Normally, by then the winning candidate had been declared, and the losing candidate had conceded.

However, in 2020, about one-third of voters— many more Democrats than Republicans—planned to cast their vote for president by mail. Some of the key "swing states," in which the election was expected to be close, were not prepared to count all the mail-in ballots quickly. And so the winner in those states, especially Pennsylvania, Michigan, and Wisconsin, might not be declared for several days. Trump, perhaps seeing an advantage for Republicans, demanded that the presidential election *must* be decided by the tallies on election night. Actually, the president had no power to enforce this demand.

As it turned out, the tallies on Tuesday evening did favor President Trump. Late that night he announced that he had won, and that he wanted "all voting" to stop. Of course all the *voting* had already taken place. But tens of millions of votes were still to be *counted*.

On Wednesday afternoon, Joe Biden stated, calmly but very firmly, "Every vote must be counted." It was not the will of Donald Trump, or of any candidate, that would determine who became the next president of the United States. It was the will of the people. "And their will alone."

This was a historic election, in that more people had cast votes for president than ever before in the history of the US. As the election workers in every state of the Union kept on counting, the mail-in ballots began shifting the numbers in Joe Biden's favor. But the results were still not clear on Wednesday night — or on Thursday. Or on Friday.

To Biden's joy, it was the state of Pennsylvania,

where he was born, that finally clinched his victory. On Saturday morning, November 7, the major TV networks announced that Biden had won Pennsylvania's twenty electoral votes, putting him over the 270 needed to win the election. The outcome in a few more states was uncertain, but Joseph R. Biden Jr. was the president-elect of the United States. He would be inaugurated as the forty-sixth president on January 20, 2021.

On Saturday evening, Kamala Harris, who would become the first female vice president as well as the first vice president of color, greeted a crowd in Wilmington so excited they could hardly stop cheering to let her speak. After her remarks, Joe Biden jogged smiling onto the stage. "I pledge to be a president who seeks not to divide, but to unify," he told the nation. He promised to work as hard for the people who had not voted for him as for those who had.

When Joe had finished speaking, his family and Kamala's family joined the victorious two on the stage. They all milled happily around, swaying to the music and watching the celebratory fireworks display.

At long last, Joseph R. Biden Jr. had achieved the dream he'd once cherished as a twelve-year-old boy.

But he was taking on an enormous task. Of all the US presidents, only Abraham Lincoln, on the brink of the Civil War, and Franklin Roosevelt, in the Great Depression and then World War II, had faced more serious crises. Joe Biden knew this, and even during the run for the White House, he had been planning how he and his team would go about running the government.

First of all, the country was deeply divided. Although more than 75 million Americans had voted to make Joe Biden the next president, more than 70 million had voted to keep Donald Trump in office. Could President Biden gain the whole country's trust? Biden would need to prove that he was president for all Americans, not only his political allies, or the people who could do him favors. Fortunately, this inclusive way of leading came naturally to Joe Biden—it was the kind of leader he'd been even as a young boy.

Then there was the ongoing pandemic. Biden had already reached out to many experts and gathered a team ready to take charge of controlling the coronavirus. However, the Trump administration's advice and actions about COVID-19 had been so confusing that large numbers of Americans were not following the CDC guidelines. And only half of Americans said they were willing to be vaccinated—when a vaccine was available. In order for the pandemic to be controlled, a majority of Americans would need to cooperate.

Once the pandemic was under control, the national economy would be able to recover. Until then, the nation's businesses and workers, as well as the cities and states, would need ongoing support from the government. To pay for such assistance, Joe Biden proposed to cancel the tax breaks Trump had given the wealthy and to raise taxes on anyone earning more than $400,000 per year. The Biden administration would need the cooperation of Congress to pass such legislation.

Joe Biden's age was another concern, and he had said that he viewed himself as a "bridge" to a younger generation of Democratic leaders. Although Biden was fit, healthy, and unusually energetic, he was the oldest person ever to be elected US president. Even Ronald Reagan was only seventy-seven as he left office in 1989. Would Biden's health and energy hold up under the enormous strain of the presidency? In case it did not, he was confident that his vice president, Kamala Harris, was "ready to lead."

Global climate change was an issue that the Trump administration had simply denied and ignored for four years. But as if to force Americans to pay attention to this mounting threat, the West Coast had burst into flames during the last months of the 2020 presidential campaign. In California, Oregon, and Washington, forest fires swept over millions of acres, driving many thousands of people from their homes and choking the air across the entire region.

At the same time, the southeastern US was battered by hurricanes and floods, and the western half of the country suffered drought. Climate scientists agreed that the devastating fires, the rise in sea levels, and the unusually violent storms were all caused by higher global temperatures. And the rise in global temperatures was caused by increased greenhouse gases released into the atmosphere by burning fossil fuels.

The United States bore a large part of the responsibility for global climate change, being the second-biggest emitter of greenhouse gases. Joe Biden planned to launch a trillion-dollar program to replace fossil fuels in the US with clean energy. Importantly, this huge effort would also stimulate the economy, by creating millions of new jobs. Just as important, the US needed to set an example for the rest of the world.

Still another pressing problem: the United States' relations with other countries were in disarray. For many years before 2016, the US had been the country that other nations looked to for leadership. By 2020, the Trump administration had strained relationships with most of the US's traditional allies. And the US had lost the respect of many nations, especially because of Trump's mishandling of the COVID-19 pandemic. Fortunately, Joe Biden had deep expertise, from his years as senator and then as vice president, in working with other countries, and he was determined to restore the US's position in the world.

During Joe Biden's long career in public service, he had faced and overcome many challenges. But it seemed that his greatest challenges lay ahead.

# Acknowledgments

Many thanks to Karen Nagel and all the editorial and production staff at Aladdin, who polished this book and made it shine. And special thanks to my husband, Robert J. Gormley, who picked Biden for a winner early on.

# Sources

**BOOKS**

Biden, Joe. *Promise Me, Dad*. New York: Flatiron Books, 2017.

Biden, Joe. *Promises to Keep: On Life and Politics*. New York: Random House, 2007.

Cramer, Richard Ben. *What It Takes: The Way to the White House*. New York: Vintage Books, 1993.

Dye, Thomas R., and L. Harmon Ziegler. *The Irony of Democracy*. Belmont, CA: Wadsworth, 1970.

Goldstein, Joel K. *The White House Vice Presidency: The Path to Significance, Mondale to Biden*. Lawrence: University Press of Kansas, 2016.

Levingston, Steven. *Barack and Joe: The Making of an Extraordinary Partnership*. New York: Hachette Book Group, 2019.

Obama, Michelle. *Becoming*. New York: Crown, 2018.

Taylor, Paul. *See How They Run: Electing the President in an Age of Mediaocracy*. New York: Knopf, 1990.

Witcover, Jules. *Joe Biden: A Life of Trial and Redemption*. New York: HarperCollins, 2010.

Woodward, Bob. *Rage*. New York: Simon & Schuster, 2020.

**MAGAZINES AND NEWSPAPERS**

Associated Press. "In Florida, Trump Goes Back on Campaign Trail." *Boston Globe*, October 13, 2020.

Ballhaus, Rebecca, Sadie Gurman, and Dustin Volz. "Rough Transcript Shows Trump Pressed Ukraine to 'look into' Joe Biden's Son." *The Wall Street Journal*, September 25, 2019.

Bidgood, Jess. "Vote Count Drama Ends with Home State Victory." *Boston Globe*, Nov. 8, 2020.

Blake, Aaron. "4 Takeaways from the Final Night of the Democratic National Convention." *The Washington Post*, August 20, 2020.

Bouie, Jamelle. "Trump's Perverse Campaign Strategy." *New York Times*, September 16, 2020.

Bowden, Mark. "The Salesman." *The Atlantic*, October 2010.

Cohn, Nate. "Large Polling Leads Tend to Erode. Is 2020 Different?" *New York Times*, July 21, 2020.

Dreier, Peter. "Don't Add Reagan's Face to Mount Rushmore." *Free Lance-Star*, April 3, 2011.

Ember, Sydney, and Jonathan Martin. "Joe Biden, in Video, Says He Will Be 'More Mindful' of Personal Space." *New York Times*, April 3, 2019.

# SOURCES

Entous, Adam. "Will Hunter Biden Jeopardize His Father's Campaign?" *New Yorker*, July 8 and 15, 2019.

Estepa, Jessica. "Joe Biden on Hillary Clinton: 'I Never Thought She Was a Great Candidate.'" *USA Today*, May 19, 2017.

Flegenheimer, Matt, and Alexander Burns. "Kamala Harris Makes the Case That Joe Biden Should Pass the Torch to Her." *New York Times*, June 27, 2019.

Glueck, Katie. "Biden Confronts Trump on Chaos and Leadership." *New York Times*, September 1, 2020.

Glueck, Katie, Thomas Kaplan, and Reid J. Epstein. "'Gasoline on the Fire': Biden Says That Trump Is Rooting for Violence." *New York Times*, August 28, 2020.

Goldmacher, Shane, and Jonathan Martin. "President Spurns Norms to Elevate Candidacy, But Virus's Reality Stays." *New York Times*, August 27, 2020.

Herndon, Astead W., and Jonathan Martin. "On King Holiday, Democrats Convey Hope, Remorse and Invective Against Trump." *New York Times*, January 21, 2019.

Kristof, Nicholas. "'I Keep My Promises,' Trump Said. Let's Check." *New York Times*, September 6, 2020.

Levey, Noam N. "Biden's Regular Joe Side." *Los Angeles Times*, August 24, 2008.

Martin, Jonathan, and Alexander Burns. "Biden Beats Trump: Race Is Finally Called after Record Turnout; Chaotic Term Ends with Rare Incumbent Loss." *New York Times*, November 8, 2020.

Martin, Jonathan, and Alexander Burns. "Biden Builds an Edge in Crucial States as Trump Challenges the Vote Counts." *New York Times*, November 5, 2020.

Martin, Jonathan, and Astead W. Herndon. "Harris Joins Biden Ticket, Achieving a First." *New York Times*, August 12, 2020.

Pierce, Charles P. "Trump's Coronavirus Bungling Has Only Boosted Joe Biden's Return-to-Normalcy Campaign." *Esquire*, March 10, 2020.

Senior, Jennifer. "Learning to Love Joe Biden." *New York Times*, August 16, 2020.

Skalka, Liz. "Biden Makes Appeal to Union Workers During Ohio Stop." *Pittsburgh Post-Gazette*, October 12, 2020.

Tomasky, Michael. "Biden's Journey Left." *New York Review of Books*, July 2, 2020.

Yuan, Jada, and Annie Linskey. "Jill Biden Is Finally Ready to Be First Lady. Can She Help Her Husband Beat Trump?" *Washington Post*, August 17, 2020.

Zimmer, Carl. "The First Covid Vaccine Will Not Make Things Normal." *New York Times*, October 13, 2020.

## INTERNET
Abutaleb, Yasmeen, and Laurie McGinley. "Here's How Joe Biden Would Combat the Pandemic If He Wins the Election." WashingtonPost.com, September 11, 2020.

# SOURCES

Allen, Terina. "Urgent Call for Second Stimulus Checks and Economic Stimulus Relief." Forbes.com, October 11, 2020.

Bartash, Jeffry. "US Economy Plunges at Titanic 32% Rate in Second Quarter and Points to Drawn-Out Recovery." Economic Report, MarketWatch.com, July 30, 2020.

BBC.com. "Covid: US Death Toll Passes 200,000." September 23, 2020.

Biden, Joe. "Public Greeting to the National Stuttering Association." National Stuttering Association, July 9, 2009. Web.Archive.org/web/20110728173845/http://www.westutter.org /pdfs/Joe_Biden-PublicGreeting_NationalStutteringAssoc_7.1.09.pdf.

Biden, Joe. "Statement by Vice President Joe Biden on the Deadly Violence in Portland." JoeBiden.com.

Bradner, Eric. "Biden Sharpens Contrast with Trump: 'I Won't Traffic in Fear and Division.'" CNN.com, June 2, 2020.

Bradner, Eric, and Sarah Mucha. "Biden Says He Is a 'Bridge' to 'New Generation' of Future Leaders." CNN.com, March 9, 2020.

Bush, Daniel, and Lisa Desjardins. "What 74 Former Biden Staffers Think About Tara Reade's Allegations." PBS.org, May 15, 2020.

CBS Chicago/CBS News/AP. "FBI Foils Militia Plot to Kidnap Michigan Gov. Gretchen Witmer, Try Her for 'Treason.'" October 8, 2020. Chicago.CBSLocal.com.

CDC.gov. "When You Can Be Around Others After You Had or Likely Had COVID-19." September 10, 2020.

CNN.com. "Read: Whistleblower Complaint Regarding President Trump and Ukraine." CNN.com, September 26, 2019.

*Congressional Record: Senate.* "An Interview with Senator Joe Biden." Congressional Record, October 2, 1975. https://int.nyt.com/data/documenthelper/1405-1975-biden-congressional-recor/07ef21b7a4b4639554d3/optimized/full.pdf.

Crowley, Michael. "Trump Won't Commit to 'Peaceful' Post-Election Transfer of Power." NYTimes.com, September 23, 2020.

Dale, Daniel. "Fact Check: Trump Makes Series of Egregious False Claims in Election Night Address." CNN.com. November 4, 2020.

Dawsey, Josh, Ashley Parker, Colby Itkowitz, and Toluse Olorunnipa. "Trump Goes to Walter Reed Hospital for Coronavirus Treatment." WashingtonPost.com, October 3, 2020.

Devlin, Kat. "International Relations Experts and U.S. Public Agree: America Is Less Respected Globally." Pew Research Center, December 17, 2018. PewResearch.org.

Ember, Sydney. "Bernie Sanders Drops Out of 2020 Democratic Race for President." NYTimes.com, April 8, 2020.

Fox, Maggie. "Here's Why a Vaccine Will Not Stop the Covid-19 Pandemic Right Away." CNN.com, September 15, 2020.

# SOURCES

Gambino, Lauren. "Joe Biden Sweeps Key Primaries and Moves Closer to Nomination." TheGuardian.com, March 18, 2020.

Glueck, Katie. "Biden Confronts Trump on Safety: 'He Can't Stop the Violence.'" NYTimes .com, August 31, 2020.

Goldmacher, Shane. "Biden Creates Legal War Room, Preparing for a Big Fight Over Voting." NYTimes.com, September 14, 2020.

Goldmacher, Shane. "Six Takeaways from the First Presidential Debate." NYTimes.com, September 30, 2020.

Itkowitz, Colby, Annie Linskey, Matt Viser, Michael Scherer, Felicia Sonmez, and John Wagner. "Biden Takes Questions and Criticizes Trump in Drive-In Town Hall; Trump Holds Rally in Wis." WashingtonPost.com, September 17, 2020.

JoeBiden.com. "The Biden Plan to Build a Modern, Sustainable Infrastructure and an Equitable Clean Energy Future." JoeBiden.com/clean-energy.

John, Arit. "An Unlikely Friendship: Cindy McCain Speaks of Her Late Husband's Relationship with Joe Biden." LATimes.com, August 18, 2020.

Kennedy, Lesley. "What Led to Desegregation Busing—and Did It Work?" History.com, July 9, 2019.

Lemon, Jason. "What the Polls Say About Donald Trump vs. Joe Biden Election." Newsweek.com, March 9, 2020.

Lord, Debbie. "Election 2020: When Does Early Voting Begin; Which States Do It?" Fox23 .com, September 3, 2020.

Malinconico, MaryAnn Love. "Pennsylvania Anthracite Culm Heaps: A Burning Issue." Carbonacea.blogspot.com (scientific blog focusing on geologic carbon), March 9, 2015.

Manchester, Julia. "The Hill's Campaign Report: Biden Picks Harris as Running Mate." TheHill.com, August 11, 2020.

McCarthy, Tom, Lauren Aratani, and agencies. "Trump Claims CDC Director Is 'Confused' over 2021 Vaccine Timetable." TheGuardian.com, September 16, 2020.

Mikelionis, Lukas. "Joe Biden's Mind 'Totally in the Clear' Despite 1988 Aneurysm, His Brain Surgeon Says." FoxNews.com, April 26, 2019.

Montanaro, Domenico. "Poll: Biden Maintains Lead over Trump with Likely Voters." NPR .org, September 18, 2020.

Montellaro, Zach, and David Siders. "How Biden Could End 2020 on Election Night—and Why Trump's Path Is Unlikely." Politico.com, October 12, 2020.

NBC News. "Former Vice President Joe Biden Front-Runner in Race for Democratic Nomination." NBC News, December 19, 2019. www.WPSDLocal6.com.

*New York Times.* "Covid World Map: Tracking the Global Outbreak." NYTimes.com.

# SOURCES

Parlapiano, Alicia. "Are You a U.S. Citizen? How a 2020 Census Question Could Affect States." NYTimes.com, March 30, 2018.

Real Clear Politics. "General Election: McCain vs. Obama." RealClearPolitics.com.

Riechmann, Deb. "AP Explains: Is a Trump White House Acceptance Speech Legal?" AP-News.com, August 6, 2020.

Saul, Stephanie. "Politics, Money, Siblings: The Ties Between Joe Biden and Valerie Biden Owens." NYTimes.com, February 25, 2020.

Schreckinger, Ben. "James Biden's Health Care Ventures Face a Growing Legal Morass." Politico.com, March 9, 2020.

Silva, Christianna. "Food Insecurity in the U.S. by the Numbers." NPR.org, September 27, 2020.

Singh, Maanvi, Tom McCarthy, and Martin Belam. "Biden Tells White Supremacist Groups to 'Cease and Desist' after Trump's Debate 'Embarrassment'—as It Happened." TheGuardian.com, October 5, 2020.

Singman, Brooke. "Trump Campaign Expects 'Tuned in' Joe Biden on Debate Night." FoxNews.com, September 28, 2020.

Sprunt, Barbara. "Biden and Trump Visit Minnesota as the State Begins Early Voting." NPR .org, September 18, 2020.

Spychalsky, Alexandra. "Who Is Maisy Biden? Joe Biden's Granddaughter Has a Tight Bond with Sasha Obama." Bustle.com, January 17, 2017.

Swasey, Benjamin. "Map: Mail-In Voting Rules by State—and the Deadlines You Need." NPR.org, October 14, 2020.

Tamari, Jonathan, and Julia Terusso. "How Joe Biden Won Pennsylvania." Inquirer.com. November 8, 2020.

Totenberg, Nina. "170 Days and Counting: GOP Unlikely to End Supreme Court Blockade Soon." NPR.org, September 6, 2016.

United States Census 2020. "What Is the 2020 Census?" 2020census.gov/en/what-is-2020-census.html.

Vogel, Kenneth P. "Trump, Biden and Ukraine: Sorting Out the Accusations." NYTimes.com, September 22, 2019.

Wallace, Gregory. "Census Bureau Says Operations Will Conclude by October 5." CNN .com, September 28, 2020.

Web.Archive.org, Information on the Violence Against Women Act. https://web.archive.org/web/20080822144642/http://biden.senate.gov/issues/issue/?id=975b0cf4-ce25-42cc-b63d-072fb81e8618.

Wike, Richard, Janell Fetterolf, and Mara Mordecai. "U.S. Image Plummets Internationally as Most Say Country Has Handled Coronavirus Badly." Pew Research Center, September 15, 2020. PewResearch.org